Praise for *A Rumor of Bl*

A Rumor of Black Lutherans finally allow
tell the story of our ancestors, innovators, and powerful elders who came before us. It outlines struggles any Black Lutheran clergy person or congregation would instantly recognize, resistance to white supremacy through the means of grace provided by the church, and hope in the stories laid out before us by Dr. Thomas's loving and careful scholarship. Whole stories for whole people—that's what's offered in this volume.

—Rev. lenny duncan, PhD student, Graduate Theological Seminary, Berkeley, California

Beyond the very rumor of biblical angels themselves, could there possibly be any rumor more timely or more fitting for North American Lutherans to hear, read, mark, learn, and inwardly digest than *A Rumor of Black Lutherans*! Years into the future, many will remain indebted, myself first of all, to Professor James Thomas for rendering public these ten profiles in courage at a time when such a dearth of leadership seems evident at nearly every turn.

—Rev. Dr. Gary M. Simpson, professor emeritus of systematic theology and emeritus Northwestern Lutheran Theological Seminary Chair of Theology, Luther Seminary

James Thomas's book provides a welcome contribution to a long-overlooked subject, the history of African American leaders within the larger story of Lutherans in America. Through ten brief biographies of individuals who lived between the eighteenth and twenty-first centuries, he illuminates this often-invisible history, emphasizing the ministry and witness of these pioneers in a church that often barely acknowledged their presence. This work is a thoughtful contribution that both broadens our understanding of what constitutes Lutheran history and contributes to contemporary discussions about Lutheran identity, culture, and context.

—Dr. Susan Wilds McArver, H. George Anderson Professor of Church History, Lutheran Theological Southern Seminary

As provocative as it is informative, James Thomas's *A Rumor of Black Lutherans* serves as a painful reminder of the role white mainline denominationalism has played in giving divine sanction to Black subordination. In paying homage to the ten profiles in courage selected for the work, Thomas reminds us of the continual tragedy/triumph nature of the African American journey. It has been tragic in the sense that even our most cherished religious symbols have made their way into the legitimation of white privilege. The triumph lies in the protracted yet redemptive struggle of these stalwart figures to overcome that legitimation by choosing human dignity over staid genuflecting, and in so doing, choosing freedom over bondage. Those with a deep concern for the current pretensions to post-racialism and how Christian faith can rediscover its liberating conscience will find this work a remarkable treasure.

—Dr. Harry H. Singleton III, former professor of religion and theology, Benedict College, Columbia, South Carolina; instructor in African American studies and religious studies, University of South Carolina

A Rumor of Black Lutherans is a silver tapestry on the stuff of leadership, or what notable author Dr. James Thomas recalls of Willie Lawrence Herzfeld: "artful, sometimes angry, resourceful." It is real. These chapters beautifully articulate lives of courage, resilience, faithfulness, tenacity, and innovation. Individual narratives are blended in a way that reveals a disposition to community that Daniel Payne, the first African American Lutheran president, yearned for in his early experience at Gettysburg Seminary: "More than 600 miles from the place of my nativity. Among strangers, among benefactors, but not among friends in the strict sense of that word." This work is part history; it is also incarnational theology.

There are lessons to take from the volume, and Thomas allows the reader to see them in stark relief. One of these is how our *readiness* to receive leadership is otherwise than leaders who will find a way *anyhow*. Multitudes of decades stepping into conflict, breakthroughs and saved lives in Alabama through the triumphs of Rosa Young, Nelson Trout's early work with the LGBTQIA+ community. There is something here for all of us. *A Rumor of Black Lutherans* is an opening to a discovery. Thomas invites the reader to walk through these pages and assess the rumor yourself.

—Dr. Michael Reid Trice, PhD, Spehar-Halligan Professor and founding director of the Center for Ecumenical and Interreligious Engagement, Seattle University

A Rumor of Black Lutherans

A Rumor of Black Lutherans

THE FORMATION OF BLACK LEADERSHIP IN EARLY AMERICAN LUTHERANISM

James R. Thomas

FORTRESS PRESS
Minneapolis

A RUMOR OF BLACK LUTHERANS
The Formation of Black Leadership in Early American Lutheranism

Library of Congress Cataloging-in-Publication Data

Names: Thomas, James (Reverend), author.
Title: A rumor of Black Lutherans : the formation of Black leadership in early American Lutheranism / James Thomas.
Description: Minneapolis, MN : Fortress Press, [2024] | Includes bibliographical references and index.
Identifiers: LCCN 2023045845 (print) | LCCN 2023045846 (ebook) | ISBN 9781506486185 (print) | ISBN 9781506486192 (ebook)
Subjects: LCSH: African American Lutherans--History. | Lutheran Church--Clergy. | Lutheran Church in America--History. | Lutheran Church--United States--History.
Classification: LCC BX8060.B53 (print) | LCC BX8060.B53 (ebook) | DDC 284.1092/396073--dc23/eng/20231220
LC record available at https://lccn.loc.gov/2023045845
LC ebook record available at https://lccn.loc.gov/2023045846

Cover image: Schomburg Center for Research in Black Culture, Photographs and Prints Division, The New York Public Library. "Family worship in a plantation in South Carolina" New York Public Library Digital Collections. Accessed May 17, 2022. https://digitalcollections.nypl.org/items/b1dd3bd3-ae7e-dc5d-e040-e00a1806309d
Cover design: Marti Naughton

Print ISBN: 978-1-5064-8618-5
eBook ISBN: 978-1-5064-8619-2

To my mom, Francis Susan Allen

CONTENTS

PREFACE

Combining a slender stalk with another does not yield two slender stalks but a more substantial one. The history of the African descent community's engagement with Lutheranism in the United States is slim. This book is a slender stalk that weaves a more comprehensive narrative of the intricate dynamics between the US Lutheran and the African descent community.

Research into African descent participation in the Lutheran Church in the United States has concentrated almost entirely on milestones or lauding mission efforts of Lutheran movements. African and African descent theologians, pastors, and lay persons discussed various themes in Lutheran theology and contemporary issues at the Conference of International Black Lutherans in Zimbabwe in 1986.[1] While these essays touch upon the formation of church workers, the writers were clearly on other errands. Here, we report and reflect on the role of US Lutheranism in African American post-secondary education since the late nineteenth century using short biographies. The biographies go beyond education and into ministry vocations. In this context, we encounter individuals psychologist Carl Jung calls "wounded healers."[2] These narratives recount the anguish of individuals who persevered, enduring wounds and suffering amid adversity, obstruction, and oppression. The narratives shed light on the prevalence of segregation, discriminatory practices, and the enduring persistence of structural inequality within the church. Black Lutheran church workers struggled to cope with these experiences, adopting what psychologist Elliot Aronson called "cognitive dissonance"—whereby individuals simultaneously hold two cognitions that are psychologically inconsistent.[3] The experience of Jehu Jones Jr., the first African descent pastor ordained by the Lutheran Church in the United States, is a painful example of a Black man who lived with opposing, conflicting actions, beliefs, attitudes, and conditions. How whites responded to Jehu Jones Jr. reflected how whites responded to the dilemma of Blacks in American life. The wounds are acknowledged while also pointing to the communities that offered solace and restoration.

Special attention is directed toward parochial elementary and high school education, as they illuminate the biographies. The book includes the educational experience drawn from the US Virgin Islands. While Denmark owned the Virgin Islands during most of the period covered in this book, Sister Emma Frances, who attended Deaconess training in Germany and at the Lutheran Deaconess Motherhouse in Philadelphia, strongly influenced a New York congregation and became the first Black deaconesses recognized by US Lutherans.

The role of US Lutheranism is clarified by (1) describing the earliest educational ventures between white Lutherans and African Americans, (2) reviewing the roles played by selected significant figures, and (3) through oral interviews of selected African Americans who studied in Lutheran schools.

The profiles presented in this book are of persons who answered the call of Jesus Christ. They prepared to work in churches, social service agencies, seminaries, and nonprofit organizations. They were educators, pastors, a deaconess, and bishops. They understood themselves to be servants of God. Some readers will see the familiar and find themselves in these short biographies. Others may unpack the unfamiliar. All should move from these pages with a deep appreciation and value for the sacred lives presented in this book.

Notes

1. Albert Pero and Ambrose Moyo. *Theology and the Black Experience: The Lutheran Heritage Interpreted by African & African-American Theologians* (Minneapolis: Augsburg Fortress Publishing House, 1988).
2. Claire Dunne. *Carl Jung Wounded Healers of the Soul* (New York: Watkins Press, 1983), 25.
3. *Elliot Aronson*. "The Theory of Cognitive Dissonance: A Current Perspective." *Advances in Experimental Psychology*, Vol. 4, 1969, 1–34.

CHAPTER 1

Jehu Jones Jr.

The First African American Lutheran Clergyperson

> The flower of my life has been devoted to your service—and while I lament a thousand imperfections which have attended my ministry; yet if I am not deceived, it has been my hearty desire to do something for the salvation of your souls.[1]

In 1832, a year after Nat Turner's insurrection in Virginia, the first African American was ordained a pastor in the Lutheran Church in the United States. Jehu Jones Jr. discerned that he "had received a call from God" to serve as a missionary in Liberia.[2] Jehu joined St. John's Lutheran Church in Charleston, South Carolina in 1829.[3]

The pastor of St. John's, John Bachman received permission from congregational leaders to invite Blacks as members in 1816. Jehu was part of a growing number of free Blacks in the congregation. Free Black membership was estimated at 40 percent at St. John's over Bachman's 56-year term, with some two thousand baptisms.[4] In 1865, of fifty-four Blacks baptized as Lutherans in South Carolina, Bachman was responsible for forty-four. The Black membership at St. John's was "the largest among Lutheran churches in the South" with almost two hundred communicants and one hundred and fifty students in Sunday school.[5] During the antebellum period, Bachman was able to attract a larger number of Black people to his congregation than any other Southern Lutheran minister.

Jehu's membership in a white Christian denomination was not unusual. By the mid-nineteenth century, thousands of enslaved and free Blacks, attracted by the theological content and the political power of Christian baptism, made their way into white churches. In the same churches, both Black and white Christians worshipped together, but within the context of white supremacy. When free Black people joined white churches, the white congregation adjusted their approach. They began including people based on their racial identity rather than their status as baptized people of God. Whites then created a new language of exclusion that was based on whiteness. This language can be seen in many aspects of church life, such as a predominantly white Jesus narrative and the use of images and language that reinforced white supremacy. At St. John's, segregation was enforced with the seating of Jehu and other Blacks in an upstairs gallery where white worshippers could not see them. By using this language and practice, white people in the church were able to create a culture that restricted Blacks and reinforced the view that whiteness was the norm and standard to which all other cultures should aspire.

Early Life

Born in 1786, Jehu was the child of Jehu Jones Sr. and Abigail Jones, both "free persons of color."[6] Having gained tailoring skills from his master Christopher Rogers, Jehu Jones Sr. purchased his freedom by manumission in 1798.[7] The Jones family was well-established in Charleston. They were members of St. Philips Episcopal Church. Jehu Jones Sr. was a significant businessman in the community. In 1815 he purchased a hotel at a public auction for $13,000.[8] Situated near St. Michael's Episcopal Church on Broad Street, the hotel occupied one of the most prominent locations in Charleston.[9] Jones Sr. began the tradition of fine hotels that catered to the white elite in a city now famous for the hospitality industry.[10] The Jones hotel was patronized by the wealthy of white society, including the governor of South Carolina.[11] Mr. Jones "lived in every way like a white man. His house was unquestionably the best in the city and had a widespread reputation."[12] Tax Records for the State of South Carolina in 1809 indicate that both Jehu Jones Sr. and Jehu Jones Jr. paid state taxes.[13] Jones Sr. also purchased enslaved people to work in his various enterprises.

Many formerly enslaved persons owed a debt of gratitude to Jehu Jones Sr. because he purchased their freedom.[14] In 1790, Jehu Jones Sr., James Mitchell, and two other men, all mulatto members of Charleston's

Image 1.1. Building Housing the Jehu Jones Hotel as it appeared in 1928. Located at 71 Broad Street, Charleston, SC.

Source: Courtesy South Carolina Historical Society.

St. Phillips Episcopal Church, established the Brown Fellowship Society (the "Brown" referring to their almost white complexion). The Brown Fellowship Society was one of the first insurance ventures among African Americans. The mission of the Brown Fellowship Society was to support African American members, widows, and children. Still, it represented classism and elitism among African Americans in Charleston. Usually, only lighter-skinned free African Americans were allowed to join.[15] Skin color differences often divided the Black community.

The Jones family's good life remained until the Denmark Vesey Rebellion (1822), Nat Turner's revolt (1831), and growing sectional crisis disturbed the harmony. The Vesey rebellion was perhaps the largest slave revolt in United States history. The rebellion failed when two slaves, George Wilson and Rolla Bennett, revealed the plan to their owners. Vesey was captured on June 21 and hanged on the morning of July 2. Emanuel African Methodist Episcopal Church in Charleston, where Vesey was a member and lay leader, was burned down. Emanuel Church later reopened after the war. In 2015, the church gained headlines again as the site of Dylann Roof's slaughter of nine African Americans at a Bible study. After the rebellion, a new series of laws was passed by Charleston authorities restricting the lives of enslaved people and free Blacks.[16] New Black churches were forbidden, triggering the building of an arsenal and guardhouse known as The Citadel. The Citadel stood in a neighborhood of free Blacks, working-class whites, and enslaved people, providing a visible reminder of city authority. The original purpose of The Citadel was to dissuade future rebellions.[17] The Citadel, the Military College of South Carolina, traces its origins to the arsenal constructed by the state of South Carolina to defend white Charlestonians against possible slave uprisings following Denmark Vesey's thwarted rebellion of 1822.

Events following the Denmark Vesey conspiracy of 1822 affected the Jones family. Free African Americans—whether part of the elite Black society or not—were closely scrutinized and subjected to stricter regulations. Adult African American men were supposed to be supervised by a white guardian. Free Black South Carolinians were not allowed to travel out of the state (and were barred from returning to the state if they traveled after the conspiracy) unless they sought express permission from the state government. Abagail Jones, Jehu's mother, was traveling with her children and grandchildren in New York before 1822 and faced difficulty returning home, ultimately dying in New York.[18] Jehu Jones Sr. died in 1833. He left an estate estimated at $40,000 (equivalent in purchasing power to about $1,322,291 in 2023)[19] to his three sons and stepdaughter, Ann Dees.

Before Jehu Jr. followed his father into the tailoring business, he and his brother Edward obtained a substantial amount of formal elementary education through their relationships with white church leaders. This highlighted the complex and ambiguous relationships between white Christians and free Blacks. The Antebellum religious views within slave-holding communities defended the institution of slavery as a divinely decreed fulfillment of God's ordering of human societies. For example, John Bachman, the pastor of Jehu's church, owned a slave. When Bachman traveled to South Carolina in 1814, he took one of the family slaves, Lydia to serve him.[20] "When the Declaration of Independence was promulgated in 1776, a London newspaper described a South Carolina clergyman reading the document aloud while being fanned by a slave."[21] Christians developed elaborate biblical defenses to justify the institution. Free Blacks in South Carolina, like Jehu and his family, continued to live with the constant fear, anxiety, and painful reality of slavery. Their lives were progressively bounded, especially during times of social instability. New laws following the Denmark Vesey conspiracy established fines and enslavement for Blacks leaving the state and attempting to return. Blacks were unable to travel or congregate freely. Many challenges faced Blacks in forming and sustaining churches, schools, or freemasonry lodges. There were also efforts by whites to evangelize free Blacks in the urban center of Charleston. While Blacks were allowed to worship with whites, white parishioners sat in the front seats and received communion first. Black people could minister to Blacks, but rarely did Blacks minister to whites. White preachers believed they could maintain paternalistic and humane practices within the oppressive environment of slavery. Free Blacks, however, often used the message and structure of paternalistic Christianity to advance and attain a measure of autonomy. During and after the end of slavery, African Americans organized congregations, parishes, fellowships, associations, and later denominations.

Theological Education

The Jones brothers were good candidates for higher education. Jehu's brother, Edward Jones, (*ca.* 1808–1864) was the first African American to graduate from Amherst College, Amherst, MA. He was a member of the Class of 1826.[22] He then studied at Andover Theological Seminary and the Episcopal Church-sponsored African Mission School Society. Edward was ordained an Episcopal priest by Bishop Thomas C. Brownwell on August 8, 1830.

Although educated for mission work in Liberia, Edward was prohibited from serving there because of a question of his "loyalty to the cause of Liberia and to the Colonization Society, with which the mission school was so intimately associated."[23] Jones held antislavery opinions dissimilar to his mission sponsors in the African Mission School. He eventually settled in Sierra Leone. Edward was the first naturalized citizen of Sierra Leone, although he retained his American citizenship. Edward became the first principal of the Fourah Bay Christian

Image 1.2. Mask and Wig Club of the University of Pennsylvania. The building founded as St. Paul's Lutheran Church, 1834; remodeled into clubhouse 1894, altered 1901-03. The building is located at 310 South Quince Street in Philadelphia.

Source: Library of Congress, Prints & Photographs Division, PA,51-PHILA,551-1.

Institution, founded in 1827,[24] and the forerunner of Fourah Bay College. Fourah Bay (located in a suburb of Freetown) became the University of Sierra Leone in 2005.

In contrast, Jehu Jones Jr., acquired his limited theological education from Pastor John Bachman at St. John's Lutheran Church. Bachman employed an apprenticeship model in his approach.[25] Informal theological education was provided for Jehu.[26] In addition to Jehu, Bachman encouraged and aided Daniel Payne (see chapter 2) and Boston Drayton (see chapter 3), Black men who worshipped at St. John's, to enter the ministry.

Lutherans in the United States did not enroll a Black person as a student at a Lutheran seminary until 1835, when Daniel Payne entered the Lutheran Theological Seminary at Gettysburg, Pennsylvania. The ordination of Black Lutherans also did not follow a progressive line of cumulative development. Ordinations grew in fits and starts, partly due to the lack of robust support for Black education in US Lutheranism. Historical records do not suggest that Rev. John Bachman urged Jehu to pursue a college or seminary education.[27] However, Bachman endorsed the endeavors of Jehu and others who aspired to join the Lutheran ministry.

The record of Bachman's preparation for the Lutheran ministry is unclear and marked by fits and starts. Bachman's early study of the Bible came through his home life. Bachman received tutoring from Lutheran pastors Anthon T. Braun and Frederick Henry Quitman.[28] "When the time arrived for John Bachman to enter college, Williams College, Massachusetts, was selected."[29] Early in his college career, a medical emergency, a hemorrhage of the lungs, forced him to leave college without graduating. Bachman next entered a college in Philadelphia, but an attack of tuberculosis forced him to withdraw. He later studied theology in Philadelphia and became a Lutheran pastor in 1813.[30] In Philadelphia, Bachman met Alexander Wilson, an American ornithologist. Wilson convinced Bachman he could serve God and pursue natural history studies.[31] Bachman recognized by the early 1820s that formal education was the future wave. He pointed out that the modern nineteenth century required a more contemporary system of educating its professionals. He was a proponent of secular and religious education and helped found Newberry College and the Lutheran Theological Southern Seminary.

Pastoral Work

In 1832, Reverend Bachman concluded that Jehu was sufficiently prepared for ordination. He penned a letter of recommendation for Jehu to colleagues in New York City because he thought that perhaps "Southern Lutherans would not agree to ordain a black man."[32] Additionally, he secured several letters of support from Charleston business leaders. With these papers in hand, Jehu departed the South for New York, seeking ordination by the New York Lutheran Ministerium.

Before sailing to New York City for ordination in 1832, Jehu, acted as executor of the estate of Barbara Maria Bampfield, wife of George Bampfield, and a free African American "residing in Guignard Street" in Charleston. As executor of the Bampfield estate, "Jones sold Bampfield's slave Fatima for $200 and divided the proceeds among Sarah Cole and Elizabeth Maria Jones."[33] Free Black people enslaved people "in each of the thirteen original states and later in every state that countenanced slavery,"[34] at least since Anthony Johnson and his wife Mary went to court in Virginia in 1654 to obtain the services of their indentured servant, a Black man, John Castor, for life. And for a time, free Black people could even own the services of white indentured servants in Virginia. Free Blacks owned enslaved people in Boston by 1724 and Connecticut by 1783; by 1790, forty-eight black people in Maryland owned 143 enslaved people. One particularly notorious Black Maryland farmer named Nat Butler "regularly purchased and sold Negroes for the Southern trade."[35] Jehu Jones Jr. belongs in the company of free Black people in the United States who bought or sold other Black people.

When Jehu arrived in New York City on October 24, 1832, with letters from John Bachman and South Carolina business leaders, he found that the Ministerium had already adjourned. Several pastors were still present at the Evangelical Lutheran Church of St. Matthews, the meeting site. According to the minutes of the Ministerium, "they took it upon themselves to 'assemble together as a self-constituted body' in order to arrive at a 'decisive and instant action.'"[36] They approved Jehu for ordination. The Ministerium reviewed and confirmed the action taken by the several pastors the following year.[37] The pastors examined Jones's theology and approved him for ordination, intending that Jones deploy as a missionary to Liberia. The letter of his ordination reads,

> Be it known to all whom these presents shall come, that we, the undersigned members of the Evangelical Lutheran Synod of the State of New York and adjacent parts, have on this day [October 24, 1832], and in the Evangelical Lutheran Church of St. Matthews, in the City of New York, after due examination, ordain Jehu Jones, Jun., a colored student of divinity, as a minister of the gospel of Our Lord and Saviour Jesus Christ, by the imposition of hands and other customary solemnities.

> Witness our hands and the affixed seal of the United German Lutheran Churches in the City of New York. [Signed by] F. W. Geisenhaimer, D.D., F. W. Geisenhaimer, Jr., Pastor of United German Lutheran Church, New York, Henry J. Smith, Charles A. Smith and Wm. D. Strobel, Pastor of St. James Church of N.Y.[38]

Reverend Bachman's recommendation of Jehu was made with the view of his serving in the Colony of Liberia, Africa. As he returned to Charleston "to help his family prepare for the trip and to set his financial house in order"[39] for his departure to Liberia, he was arrested for breaking a South Carolina law, *The Negro Seaman's Act of 1822*.[40] The Negro Seaman's Act made it mandatory that free seamen of African descent working aboard foreign or domestic ships be jailed and held prisoner when the ship entered any of South Carolina's harbors. These persons were detained until their ship was ready to sail. A $1,000 per person court fee had to be paid by the vessel's captain. Failure to pay these costs made the captain liable to two months imprisonment. Unclaimed seamen were sold into slavery, even if they were foreign nationals. The purpose of the law, later imitated in Louisiana, North Carolina, Alabama, Georgia, Florida, and Texas, was to inhibit the interaction of enslaved people with free seamen. The law of 1822 was enforced in South Carolina until the Civil War.[41] Jehu was released on the condition that he never return to South Carolina.[42]

On his release from jail, Jones returned to New York City. He promptly arranged for his family to travel to New York. Pastor Strobel from the New York synod wrote in a letter to Rev. S. S. Schmucker that Jones raised sufficient money to

> pay their expenses . . . within $30, or $40—but it is in regard to his future destination. Particularly that he wished to lay his circumstances before you. I think that the prospects are very fair, for establishing a Lutheran Church at the colony [i.e., Liberia], almost immediately. About 250 have lately sailed from Charleston, and 3 or 400 more will follow in the spring, some of whom are members of Mr. Bachman's church, and I think it very probable, that many, who are not Lutherans, would become the adherents of Mr. Jones. From the

> circumstances of being fellow-townsmen, and most of them his acquaintances in America, is it not worthwhile to make an exertion in this business[?] Mr. J. supposes that 4 or $500 per annum, would enable him to support his family—and if the prospects are good, he would not require it long, and with a very small outfit he would be able to sail in one of the first vessels. He has made application to the American board of Commissioners for foreign Missions, but they declined doing anything for him, referred him to you personally.[43]

Though it was all set for Jehu to finally go to Liberia, in 1833 Jones met with Ralph R. Gurney in Washington, DC, and Samuel H. Cox of New York City. Both men were leaders of the American Colonization Movement.[44] Jehu learned that Lutherans in Pennsylvania were looking for a "young gentleman of education" to do mission work among Black people in New York and Philadelphia.[45] At the suggestion of Samuel Simon Schmucker,[46] the decision was made that Jehu would stay in the United States.

Jehu then settled in Philadelphia with his wife and nine children. According to Pennsylvania Synod records, he received an appointment as a missionary "among the colored people in Philadelphia under the direction of our ministers there."[47] In a letter from the Pennsylvania Synod Minutes a year later in 1834, Jehu thanked the synod for his appointment.[48] After that, Jehu began work that resulted in the organizing of St. Paul's Lutheran Church, an African American congregation. Funds for his work came through appeals in the Lutheran Observer, a biweekly newspaper. St. Paul's Church was dedicated May 1, 1836, with the Reverend Philip Mayer (Synod of Pennsylvania)[49] and the Reverend Jacob Medtart (Synod of Pennsylvania) officiating.[50]

By the time the church was dedicated in 1836, the congregation had paid nearly 40 percent of the construction costs. Appeals for support were made in the *Lutheran Observer*, and $846 was collected. Financial support was offered to Jehu by the Pennsylvania Synod with the condition that the property, deeds, and financial records be turned over to the Synod. After some hesitation, Jehu agreed on behalf of the congregation.[51] One year after an auspicious beginning, creditors demanded that the new congregation pay its bills, but Jehu failed to present the Synod with the deeds to St. Paul's Church. The Synod also failed to uphold its agreement to support the congregation financially. In 1839 Jehu reported to the Pennsylvania Ministerium that the congregation's Board of Trustees had sold the church building and that his position as pastor had been terminated. A sheriff's sale sold the structure and an adjourning lot.[52]

Jones wrote to the Pennsylvania Synod in May 1839, complaining that the Synod had failed to honor their agreement through lack of support.[53] He felt betrayed by Pastor Philip Mayer, who had assured him of synod support. Mayer and a Synod committee had promised that St. Paul's Church would eventually be received as a member of the Pennsylvania Synod. This did not happen. The Synod also provided only $100 to liquidate St. Paul's debts, stipulating that it would be dispersed only if matching funds could be solicited. Karl E. Johnson's review of these developments, while aligned with the synod, is insightful:

> In regards to the trustees, it was irregular and a breach of trust for them to sell the church property without synodical approval. Their actions eventually destroyed Jones' credibility, and it is unclear what his role was in the entire affair. He was nevertheless cited for duplicity, and mishandling of funds. St. Paul's relationship with the Lutheran Church was severely damaged. Furthermore, Jones obviously misunderstood the terms negotiated by the committee, and the Pennsylvania Ministerium. No longer exerting strong control over the congregation, and with his position as missionary not clearly validated, Jehu Jones' bitter and impassioned complaints before the Synod of 1839 alienated many of the church officials. He appealed to the General Synod that year, and to the Pennsylvania Synod in 1843, for financial support. They took no action on his request.[54]

Failing to gain the support of the General Synod and the Pennsylvania Synod, Jehu moved to Toronto, Canada. He spent 1839 to 1842 in Canada then returned to the United States, where he worked as a missionary and a cobbler. Though he wanted to return to New York, "the combination of racism and unfounded charges of financial mismanagement relative to the foreclosure of 1839 foiled his attempt to found a church in New York City."[55] However, finally in 1849, seventeen years after his ordination, Jones appealed to the New York Ministerium for funds to establish a congregation among African Americans in New York City. The Ministerium referred Jones's request to a special committee chaired by Henry N. Pohlman. The special committee issued a scathing evaluation critical of Jones's labors in Philadelphia and disavowed his legitimacy as a Lutheran church pastor. The special committee refused the request. Unacquainted with Jones's work in Philadelphia, they impugned his character determining,

> from the period of his ordination to the present time, he has never been in contact with this or any other Lutheran Ministerium; and as he represented himself to be a Lutheran missionary and under this designation has imposed himself upon the churches, making collections of money and appropriating them to his own personal use, we deem it our duty to warn the Christian public against his misrepresentations and impositions.[56]

In a rebuttal to the charge that he had not held membership in a ministerium, Jones wrote,

> As respects my not being a member of the Synod, I did not know, for several years after my ordination that I should apply for membership in that body. As soon as I was informed of the matter, I requested Dr. Strobel, my advisor and friend, to apply for me, or to direct me how. I repeated this request several times. He then said there was some prejudice against me in Dr. Mayer which was so strong nothing would be done for me.[57]

Jones continued to minister to the small and impoverished congregation of St. Paul, Philadelphia, for years. Despite these setbacks and the financial hardship Jones endured he faithfully continued in his calling as a Christian pastor. As late as 1851 Jones continued to lead his congregation, holding Sunday services at Benezet Hall on Seventh Street. The Pennsylvania Ministerium's limited resources, it's failure to embrace the religious needs of Black people, the disruption of the Civil

War, and the surge of immigrants from central and northern Europe after 1865 ended the Lutheran organized outreach to the Philadelphia African American community in the nineteenth century.

Political Life

Jehu, while concentrating on the formidable work of organizing a congregation and navigating the murky waters of US Lutheranism as the first African American Lutheran pastor, also involved himself in the larger Black community. In 1845 Jehu became politically active in Philadelphia. He teamed with Nathaniel W. Depee,[58] Benjamin Paschal, Jonathan C. Miller, and Leonard Collins to organize a convention at Temperance Hall.[59] They undertook a large "endeavor to unite the whole family of free colored people in interest and feelings, for the lawful rights to petition to the constituted authorities of our country, for the repeal of every law injurious to native-born Americans."[60] The group organized a convention in 1845 at Philadelphia's Temperance Hall, urging listeners to petition city authorities for Black civil rights. They drew up a constitution and adopted the name the Colored American National Society. Its headquarters were in Philadelphia, and a network of auxiliaries was planned across the country.

From 1851 to 1852, Jones was the proprietor of a dry goods store. He and his spouse, Elizabeth, his youngest daughter, Mary Jane, and his son-in-law, John P. Williams, lived together.

From 1851 to 1852, Jehu wrote a series entitled "Letters on the Sacraments."[61] He also wrote briefly for *The African American Repository and Colonial Journal*.[62] In 1852 Jones and his family moved to Centerville, New Jersey (now Camden). He died at age sixty-six on September 28, 1852, and was buried two days later.[63] Elizabeth Jones died in Philadelphia on October 9, 1886, at the age of ninety-five.

Jehu Jones Jr. and Lutheranism

Although the "trials"[64] of Jehu Jones Jr. might arguably not be the most joyful beginning point for the educational experience of African Americans within the context of US Lutheranism, the Jehu Jones Jr.

story illustrates that Lutherans, even those who were aware of the standards of professional development for entering the ministry, did not attempt to prepare Jehu fully for church ministry. Dr. John Bachman informally prepared Jehu for ministry and personally arranged for his ordination. William Strobel, who served as president of Hartwick Seminary, took part in a quick ordination of Jehu without a recommendation for theological education. The record indicates Dr. Samuel Schmucker, who started a seminary in his house because he was concerned for an educated white clergy, did not encourage Jehu Jones Jr. to pursue higher learning at the Gettysburg Seminary, where Schmucker filled the chair of systematic theology for forty years. Schmucker was however favorably impressed with the prospect of Jehu going to Liberia and offered to support him as a missionary.

Given that Jones could not receive theological education at a Lutheran seminary, he would have benefited from enrollment at an already established African American school such as Cheney or Ashmun. Jehu, once ordained, was not mentored, or influenced, nor were attempts made to guide him toward the excellence obtainable presumably through higher education. White Lutherans failed to notice the first African American pastor in their denomination and that history was being written. Reflecting on the tragedy of Jones's experience, Catherine L. Bachman, daughter of John Bachman, offers the benign opinion that Jehu, "Had been a very useful man in his Church as a leader, and might have been so as a preacher at home (in South Carolina) where the negro characteristics and peculiarities were understood."[65] Jehu stands in sharp contrast to his brother Edward, who was the first African American to graduate from Amherst College, and who, after studies at Andover Theological Seminary, was ordained an Episcopal priest and served for thirty-four years as principal of Fourah Bay College, Sierra Leone, West Africa.

Jehu was the first African American ordained a Lutheran clergyman. He was never permitted any genuine fellowship with fellow Lutheran clergy who consistently and condescendingly referred to him as a "colored preacher." The experience of Jehu Jones Jr. is rooted in paternalism and racism. Theologian James H. Cone wrote that racism "is concealed or unconscious. The racial climate of the country has often found its most troublesome expression in the church."[66] Lutherans were not ready for the arrival of Jehu Jones Jr. Had adequate support and care been provided for Jones and were conditions different, St. Paul Lutheran Church, Philadelphia, might functionally exist today as the earliest African American Lutheran congregation in the United States.

Notes

1. Helen MacLam, "Introduction: Black Puritan on the Northern Frontier," in Richard Newman, ed., *Black Preacher to White America: The Collected Writings of Lemuel Haynes, 1774–1833* (New York: Carlson, 1990), xxxv.
2. Liberia, "land of the free," was founded by free African Americans and freed slaves from the United States in 1820. An initial group of eighty-six immigrants, who came to be called Americo-Liberians, established a settlement in Christopolis (now Monrovia, named after US President James Monroe) on February 6, 1820.

   Thousands of freed American slaves and free African Americans arrived during the following years, leading to the formation of more settlements and culminating in a declaration of independence of the Republic of Liberia on July 26, 1847. The drive to resettle freed slaves in Africa was promoted by the American Colonization Society (ACS), an organization of white clergyman, abolitionists, and slave owners founded in 1816 by Robert Finley, a Presbyterian minister. Between 1821 and 1867 the ACS resettled some ten thousand African Americans and several thousand Africans from intercepted slave ships; it governed the Commonwealth of Liberia until independence in 1847.

   In Liberia's early years, the Americo-Liberian settlers periodically encountered stiff and sometimes violent opposition from indigenous Africans, who were excluded from citizenship in the new republic until 1904. At the same time, British and French colonial expansionists encroached upon Liberia, taking over much of its territory. Politically, the country was a one-party state ruled by the True Whig Party (TWP). Joseph Jenkins Roberts, who was born and raised in America, was Liberia's first president. The style of government and constitution was fashioned on that of the United States, and the Americo-Liberian elite monopolized political power and restricted the voting rights of the indigenous majority population. The Rue Whig Party dominated all sectors of Liberia from independence in 1847 until April 12, 1980, when indigenous Liberian Master Sergeant Samuel K. Doe (from the Krahn ethnic group) seized power in a coup d'état. Doe's forces executed President William R. Robert and several officials of his government, mostly of Americo-Liberian descent. One hundred and thirty-three years of Americo-Liberian political domination ended with the formation of the People's Redemption Council (PRC). Source: US Department of State, www.state.gov/r/pa/ei/bgn/6618.htm (retrieved March 6, 2010)

3. BlackPast, Jehu Jones, Jr. (1786–1852) https://www.blackpast.org/african-american-history/jones-jehu-jr-1786–1852/. Retrieved June 16, 2019.
4. John Bachman Website, http://johnbachman.org/. Retrieved January 30, 2023
5. Bachman, *Discourse*, 8: Bachman, *John Bachman*, 354–55; *Happoldt Journal*, 35–36: Strange, "Our Duty to Preach," 174–75.
6. William C. Nell, *The Colored Patriots of the American Revolution* (New York: Arno Press and the New York Times, 1968), p. 245. See also, Karl E. Johnson, Jr. and Joseph A. Romero. "Jehu Jones (1786–1852): The First African American Lutheran Minister" in *Lutheran Quarterly* Vol. 10, 1996, 425–444. Johnson and Romero reported that Jehu Jones Sr. ". . . was a mulatto slave belonging to a white tailor named Christopher Rogers. Starting out in his master's trade, Jones, Sr. became, by dent of industry, part of the elite of Charleston's black community."
7. Manumission of Jehu Jones. Secretary of State. Recorded Instruments. Miscellaneous Records (Main Series). Volume 3Q, pp. 140, 286–287. S 213003. South Carolina Department of Archives and History, Columbia, South Carolina.

   State of South Carolina—To all to whom these Presents shall come be seen or made known I Christopher Rogers of Charleston in State aforesaid send Greeting. Know ye that I the said Christopher Rogers for and in consideration of the Sum of one hundred Pounds Sterling to me in hand well and truly paid at or before the Sealing and delivery of these presents and for divers other good causes and considerations me thereunto especially moving, have manumitted enfranchised and set free, and by these presents do manumit enfranchise and set free a certain Mulatto Man named Jehu Jones of and from all manner of bondage and Slavery whatsoever. To have and to hold such manumission and freedom unto the said Mulatto Man named Jehu Jones for ever. In Witness whereof I have hereunto set my Hand and Seal the twenty second day of January in the year of our Lord one thousand seven hundred and ninety eight-Sealed and Delivered in the Presence} Chris Rogers (LS)* of James Donaldson, Alexr. Clarkson } Charleston

   Personally appeared Mr. Alexander Clarkson who being duly sworn made oath that he was present and saw Christopher Rogers sign seal and as his Act and Deed deliver the within Deed &c&c for the uses and purposes therein set forth and that he the Deponent with James Donaldson signed their names as witnesses thereto-Sworn to the 22d day of January 1798 before Stephen Ravenel JQo Recorded 22d January 1798.

[*The (LS) or Locus Sigilli, meaning in place of seal on documents, shows the originals were signed by the individuals with their legal Signature.]

State of South Carolina
To all to whom these Presents shall come be seen or made known I Christopher Rogers of Charleston in the State aforesaid Send Greeting. Know ye that I the said Christopher Rogers for and in consideration of the Sum of One hundred Pounds Sterling to me in hand well and truly paid at or before the Sealing and Delivery of these presents and for divers other good causes and considerations me thereunto especially moving have Manumitted

443 enfranchised and set free, and by these presents do manumit enfranchise and set free a certain Mulatto Man named Jehu Jones of and from all manner of bondage and Slavery whatsoever. To have and to hold such manumission and freedom unto the said Mulatto Man named Jehu Jones forever, In Witness whereof I have hereunto set my Hand and Seal the twenty second day of January in the year of our Lord one thousand seven hundred and ninety eight

Sealed and Delivered in the presence of James Donaldson, Alex.r Clarkson — Chris. Rogers LS
Charles Cowles

Personally appeared Mr Alexander Clarkson who being duly sworn made oath that he was present and saw Christopher Rogers sign seal and as his act and Deed deliver the within Deed for the uses and purposes therein set forth and that he the Deponent with James Donaldson signed their names as Witnesses thereto — Sworn to the 22d day of January 1798 before Stephen Ravenel R.
Recorded 22d January 1798

8. John Hope Franklin, *From Slavery to Freedom* (New York: Alfred A. Knopf, 1969), 224.
9. (The Elder Jones) Register of the Mense Conveyance Office, Book M8, 21–98. Also, 399–402.
10. Harlan Greene and Stephen Hoffius. "The Charleston 100." *Charleston Magazine*, August 2008. www.charlestonmag.com/100most/20–40.html (retrieved March 6, 2010)
11. Clientele. Adams, F.C., Manuel Periera (Washington, DC, 1853), 88–89.
12. Nell, *The Colored Patriots of the American Revolution*, 244.
13. 1809—South Carolina Petition to the Senate to excuse "people of color and free Negroes" who paid property tax from also having to pay the capitation tax. Petitioners: Jehu Jones, Thomas Inglis, James Mitchell, Isaac Austin, William Clark, John Livingston, William Cooper, William Pinceel, Joseph Humphries, Phillip Manuel, Robert Hopton, Corlus Huger, James Wilson, C.G. Pinceel, George Logan, Peter Robertson, Henry Chatters, Richard Holloway, William Eden, John Martin, Morris Brown,

Abraham Jacobs, Ed Chrighton, George Chrigton, John Francis, Jehu Jones Jr., George H. Bedon, Moses Irving. http://www.raceandhistory.com/cgi-bin/forum/webbbs_config.pl?md=read;id=2248

14. Douglas C. Strange, "Trials and Tribulations of One Jehu Jones, Jr., The First Ordained Negro Lutheran Clergyman in America," *Una Sancta* 24 no. 2. (Pentecost 1967): 51–55.
15. James B. Browning, "The Beginning of Insurance Enterprise Among Negroes," *Journal of Negro History,* XXII (1937): 426.
16. Junius P. Rodriguez, ed. *Slavery in the United States: A Social, Political, and Historical Encyclopedia*, Vol. 1. (Santa Barbara, CA: ABC-CLIO, 2007), 203.
17. W. Gary Nichols, "The Citadel," *South Carolina Encyclopedia.* University of South Carolina. https://www.scencyclopedia.org/sce/entries/the-citadel/. Retrieved February 8, 2023.
18. Michael Fate, Jehu Jones, Sr. (1769–1833). Blackpast.org. https://www.blackpast.org/african-american-history/jones-jehu-sr-1769-1833/. Retrieved June 20, 2023.
19. Ian Webster. "$40,000 in 1830 to 2023/Inflation Calculator." Official Inflation Data, Aliota Finance, 13 June 2023, https://www.officialdata.org/us/inflation/1830?amount=40000. Retrieved June 30, 2023.
20. C.L. Bachman, John Bachman Haskell, and James John Audubon. *John Bachman: The Pastor of St. John's Lutheran Church, Charleston.* Smithsonian Libraries (Walker, Evans and Cogswell, 1888), 10, 17, 26, 356.
21. American Slavery and Southern Religion. August 1, 2017. https://worldhistory.us/american-history/american-slavery-and-southern-religion.php. Retrieved, January 20, 2023.
22. Amherst College Class of 1826 (from the Amherst College Biographical Record, Centennial Edition (1821–1921), http://www.amherst.edu/~rjyanco94/genealogy/acbiorecord/1826.html#jones-e. Retrieved November 7, 2011.
23. Harold T. Lewis, *Yet With Steady Beat: The African American Struggle for Recognition in the Episcopal Church.* (Valley Forge, PA: Trinity Press International, 1996), 109–121. See also: *George F. Bragg, DD,* (Wilberforce University), *History of the Afro-American Group of the Episcopal Church* (Baltimore: Church Advocate Press, 1922), 186). See also: Kenneth Walter Cameron, *American Episcopal Clergy: Registers of Ordinations in the Episcopal Church in the United States from 1785 Through 1904—With Indexes* (Hartford: Transcendental Books), 16.
24. Fourah Bay College (founded in 1827 as the first Western-style university in West Africa) is the oldest university college in West Africa. It became

the University of Sierra Leone in 1960. It is located atop Mount Aureole in Freetown, Sierra Leone.

25. Although his father, Jacob Bachman was a slave owner near the village of Rhinebeck, Dutchess County, New York, Bachman helped educate many Charlestonians of African descent—an act both illegal and socially unacceptable in the antebellum South—and is said to have baptized as many as ninety blacks in one year, helping raise the black membership of St. John's as high as 40 percent. https://en.wikipedia.org/wiki/John_Bachman, retrieved November 5, 2023.
26. The Reverend John Bachman (1790—1847) served as president of the New York Ministerium, president of the Synod of the South, and as an organizer and president of the General Synod. He served as pastor of St. John's Lutheran Church Charleston, South Carolina for 56 years. He helped found Newberry College and the Lutheran Theological Southern Seminary. Bachman collaborated with J.J. Audubon to produce *Viviparous Quadrapeds of North America.* See: Gerhard E. Lenski, *The Encyclopedia of the Lutheran Church,* Julius Bodensieck, ed., vol. A–E (Minneapolis: Augsburg Publishing House, 1963), 174.
27. Lenski, *The Encyclopedia of the Lutheran Church,* 121.
28. *A History of The Lutheran Church in South Carolina*. Published by the South Carolina Synod of the Lutheran Church in America. Columbia, SC, R.L. Bryan, 1971, 163.
29. Bachman, Haskell, and Audubon, *John Bachman*, 19.
30. Lester D. Stephens. Bachman, John—February 4, 1790—February 24, 1874. http://www.scencyclopedia.org/sce/entries/bachman-john/. Retrieved, June 16, 2019.
31. John Bachman's Personal Background: A Brief Biography (1790–1874). An on-line initiative of the Alumni Association of Newberry College, Newberry, SC. See also: Mary Bachman Hoover, *John Bachman: A Life of Service*, a short biographical sketch written in the late 1970s; https://en.wikipedia.org/wiki/John_Bachman; https://web.archive.org/web/20170926070115/http:/johnbachman.org/, retrieved, November 5, 2023. Retrieved, September 23, 2010.
32. Raymond M. Bost and Jeff L. Norris, *All One Body: The Story of the North Carolina Lutheran Synod 1803–1993* (Salisbury, NC: North Carolina Synod, Evangelical Lutheran Church in America, 1994). Bost and Norris present John Bachman, if anything, as a man of genuine contrast. Bachman served as pastor to two hundred African Americans in 1845. They were members of his congregation, St. John's Lutheran Church, Charleston. While serving the spiritual needs of African Americans he ". . . argued, contrary to some prominent scientists of the day, that the black person belonged to the human species,

(but) insisted that an examination of free blacks, both in Africa and in more fully developed societies, indicated that they were an inferior variety of the human species" (p. 92). Bachman, in response to a resolution adopted by pastors and laymen of Lawrence County (Middle Conference of the Pittsburg Synod) in 1857, ". . . provided for the most detailed defense of slavery to come from the pen of a Lutheran clergyman in the antebellum South" (p. 92). Although he held Unionist views, when South Carolina met to enact the Ordinance of Secession in December 1860, Bachman opened the meeting with a prayer (https:// web.archive.org/web/20170211222652/http://johnbachman.org/ HPersonalBackgroundMain.html). In an article published in the Charleston Medical Journal (Rev. 10:482-534, 1855, titled: *An examination of Prof. Agassiz's sketch of the natural provinces of the animal world and their relation to the different types of man, with a tableau accompanying the sketch*), Bachman, argued that the Black population was permanently and unalterably inferior to the white population, that it was incapable of self-government, that it achieved its highest state in the "protection" of the white population—i.e., slavery.

33. Paul Heinegg. *Free African Americans of North Carolina, Virginia and South Carolina,* 5th ed. (Baltimore, MD: Genealogical Publishing, 2005). See also: "Church-Cotanch," https://freeafricanamericans.com/Church-Cotanch.htm, Cole Family (South Carolina) downloaded September 23, 2010.
34. Henry Louis Gates Jr. "Did Black People Own Slaves?" *The Root.* American Renaissance. March 4, 2013. http://www.amren.com/news/2013/03/did-black-people-own-slaves/. Retrieved April 28, 2015.
35. Gates Jr., "Did Black People Own Slaves?"
36. Karl E. Johnson and Joseph A. Roemo, "Jehu Jones (1786–1852): The First African American Lutheran Minister." *Lutheran Quarterly,* 10, no. 4, (1996): 425–444.
37. Minutes, NY Ministerium, 1833, p. 17.
38. Harry J. Kreider, *History of the United Lutheran Synod of New York and New England*, vol. 1 (Philadelphia: Muhlenberg Press: 1954), 152.
39. *A History of the Lutheran Church in South Carolina*. Prepared and edited by The History of Synod Committee. Published by The South Carolina Synod, Printed by The R. L. Bryan Company, Columbia, SC. 1971, p. 268.
40. "The Negro Seaman's Act provided that sailors entering Charleston Harbor be arrested and held until their vessels sailed again. All other free Negroes entering Charleston did so under penalty of prison or the auction block." Saunders Redding, *The Lonesome Road, The Story of the Negro's Part in America* (Garden City, NY: Doubleday, 1958), 31.

41. In1823 Justice William Johnson, an Associate Justice of the US Supreme Court, invalidated the South Carolina Negro Seaman Act in *Elkison v. Deliesseline,* 8 Fed. Cas. 493, no. 4,366 (C.C.D.S.C. 1823) a case challenging the Negro Seamen Act of 1822. Johnson ruled that such an ordinance was unconstitutional because it violated the power of Congress to regulate interstate commerce, which included navigable waters. The case was not heard by the US Supreme Court. The Executive branch refused to enforce the Johnson's decision, tacitly approving South Carolina's actions and encouraging other Southern states to adopt similar exclusionary laws against people of African descent. The lack of meaningful federal intervention eventually empowered South Carolina to issue an Ordinance of Nullification, declaring federal law "utterly null and void," an act that foreshadowed the Civil War.

    Although the Supreme Court did not review the constitutionality of the Negro-Seamen Act, Johnson's decision was upheld the following year in *Gibbons v. Ogden,* (1824). In *Gibbon v. Ogdens*, the Court, declared a Maryland state law allowing a private New York enterprise to hold a monopoly on steamboat licensing and exclude out-of-state vendors, unconstitutional under the Interstate Commerce Clause and Supremacy Clause. The Court held that federal and constitutional law superseded state law and affirmed Congress's right to regulate trade between the states, including coastal and inland navigable waters. The decision furthered the United States' political agenda and was enforced, establishing a precedent that favored the federal government.

    South Carolina continued the practice of incarcerating black sailors until the Civil War. See Donald G. Morgan, *Justice William Johnson, the First Dissenter: The Career and Constitutional Philosophy of a Jeffersonian Judge* (University of South Carolina Press, June 1954).
42. Strange, *The Trials and Tribulations of One Jehu Jones, Jr.*, 51–55.
43. Lutheran Observer, 2, no. 13, February 1, 1833.
44. Eric Burin, *Slavery and the Peculiar Solution: A History of the American Colonization Society* (University Press of Florida, 2005). From the early 1700s through the late 1800s, many whites advocated removing Blacks from America. The American Colonization Society (ACS) epitomized this desire to deport Black people. Founded in 1816, the ACS championed the repatriation of African Americans to Liberia in West Africa. Supported by James Madison, James Monroe, Henry Clay, and other notables, the ACS sent thousands of Black emigrants to Liberia. In examining the ACS's activities in America and Africa, Eric Burin assesses the organization's impact on slavery and race relations.

    Burin focuses on ACS manumissions—that is, instances wherein slaves were freed on the condition that they go to Liberia. In doing so, he provides the first account of the ACS that covers the entire South throughout the antebellum era. He investigates everyone involved in the society's affairs, from the emancipators and freed persons at the center to the colonization agents, free Blacks, southern jurists, newspaper editors, neighboring whites, proslavery ideologues, northern colonizationists, and abolitionists on the periphery. In mixing a panoramic view of ACS operations with close-ups on individual participants, Burin presents a unique, bifocal perspective on the ACS.

45. Strange, *The Trials and Tribulations of One Jehu Jones, Jr.*, 51–57.
46. Samuel Simon Schmucker (1799–1873) graduated from Princeton in 1820. Ordained in 1821, he established in his own parsonage a seminary which for many years encouraged the General Synod to establish Gettysburg Seminary, the first theological school of Lutherans in the United States. On September 5, 1826, he was formally inaugurated as the first professor and for the next forty years he filled the chair of Systematic Theology, helping some five hundred young men prepare for the ministry. Schmucker was a vocal advocate of one view in the Lutheran Church that the denomination must be adapted to the American religious and political climate, especially in relationships with other churches and the matter of evangelicalism and mission.

    Schmucker, whose 1850 household, according to the Adams County census, consisted of twelve persons, including Jesse, age 70, and Clarissa, age 60, two Virginia-born former slaves that came with his second marriage and were manumitted upon moving to Pennsylvania.

    Schmucker used the Seminary, along with hidden rooms in his own basement, as a stop on the Underground Railroad, providing temporary safety for slaves fleeing bondage. See: Seminary Ridge Historic Preservation Foundation, "Preserving Legacies for Futures to Come," http://www.seminaryridge.org/legacy/Historicalstructures_files/Historical%20Structures.htm, accessed September 26, 2010.
47. Minutes of the German Evangelical Lutheran Synod of Pennsylvania. Sumneytown. Enos, Benner, June 2–6, 1833, pp. 6, 15.
48. Minutes of the German Evangelical Lutheran Synod of Pennsylvania. May 25–28, 1834.
49. Philip F. Meyer (1781?–1858). Mayer was pastor of the Evangelical Lutheran Church of St. John in Philadelphia. A native of Auburn, New York he resided in Albany before moving to Philadelphia. He served for many years as president of the Pennsylvania Institution for the Deaf and Dumb, Philadelphia Dispensary and a trustee of the University of Pennsylvania. Mayer served as a manager of the Bible Society from 1808–1858 and became the Society's third president in 1848, a position

he held until his death in 1858. Source: Pennsylvania Bible Society www.pabible.org/meetmanagers.html (Retrieved October 9, 2010.)

50. Jehu Jones Jr., "A New Lutheran Church for Colored People in Philadelphia." *Lutheran Observer*. 3, no. 37 (May 6, 1836): 147.
51. Ministerium of Pennsylvania. Minutes of the German Evangelical Lutheran Synod of Pennsylvania. (Allentown, PA: A & W Blumer, 1837), 15–16.
52. Karl E. Johnson, "Jehu Jones, Jr. and St. Paul's Evangelical Lutheran Church: A Revisionist View." *The Periodical*, Lutheran Historical Society of Eastern Pennsylvania, (April 1995): 4. See also, Second Minutes Book of the Trustees of St. John's Evangelical Lutheran Church. (The Trustees of St. Paul's Church requested aid to liquidate their outstanding debt of $2,000, April 30, 1838. In their letter they stated that the church had been slated for Sheriff's sale January 1, 1831 to January 1, 1947, pp. 69, 99–100. Lutheran Archives Center, Philadelphia, PA.
53. Jehu Jones Jr., *Letter to Pennsylvania Synod*. Lutheran Archives Center at Philadelphia. May 1839.
54. Johnson, "Jehu Jones, Jr. and St. Paul's Evangelical Lutheran Church," 2.
55. Kenneth Randolph Taylor. Sundry Thoughts. Feast of Jehu Jones (September 28) Retrieved June 17, 2019. https://neatnik2009.wordpress.com/tag/jehu-jones/
56. Kreider, *History of the United Lutheran Synod of New York and New England*, 152.
57. Jehu Jones Jr. The New York Evangelical Lutheran Synod and Rev. Jehu Jones. Philadelphia, Publisher [s.n.] 1851, pp. 1–2. See also: Minutes of the Fifty-Fourth Session of the Evangelical Lutheran Ministerium of the State of New York, and Adjacent States and Counties (Albany, NY: Joel Munsell, 1849), 19, 21.
58. Nathaniel Depee had long been active in the Philadelphia Black community. In 1845, he helped form the short-lived Colored American National Society. He was instrumental in the creation of the Vigilance Committee in late 1852 and served on its Action Committee. He was a dedicated operative in the underground railroad. In 1854, he lived at 334 South Street. Historical Society of Pennsylvania. Online collections. Journal C of Station No. 2, William Still, 1852–1857, Still Journal Text, 1853, 1853 2. (Retrieved October 10, 2010)
59. Julie Winch, *Philadelphia's Black Elite: Activism, Accommodation, and the Struggle for Autonomy, 1787–1848* (Philadelphia: Temple University Press, 1988), 202.
60. Winch, *Philadelphia's Black Elite,* 202.

61. *The Christian Observer.* March, 1850 through December, 1851.
62. "Slaves without Masters," *The African American Repository and Colonial Journal*, 15, no. 10 (June 1839): 178–180.
63. The State of Pennsylvania dedicated a historical marker in honor of the Rev. Jehu Jones, Jr. Sunday, February 22, 1998, County: Philadelphia; Marker Type: City Categories: African American, Religion Location: 310 S. Quince St., Philadelphia Marker Text: First African American Lutheran pastor in the U.S. Founder of nation's first African American Lutheran congregation, St. Paul's Evangelical Lutheran Church. It built its first brick edifice here in 1834; worshiped at this site, with Jones as its pastor, until 1839. *Black History in Pennsylvania*. http://www.portal.state.pa.us/portal/server.pt/community/resources/18089/historical_markers/617010 (Retrieved October 16, 2010.
64. Strange, *The Trials and Tribulations of One Jehu Jones, Jr.*, 51–55.
65. C. L. Bachman. *John Bachman, D.D., L.L.D, PhD.* (Charleston, 1888), 360.
66. Peter J. Thuesen. "Enclave within an Enclave: African Americans within Lutheranism, 1669–1994." Center for the Study of American Religion. Princeton University, Department of Religion. February 25, 1994, pp. 20–21.

CHAPTER 2

Daniel Alexander Payne

The First African American College President

> The Spirit of the Lord is upon me,
> Because he has anointed me to bring good news
> to the poor. He has sent me to proclaim release
> to the captives and recovery to the bling,
> to let the oppressed go free to proclaim the
> year of the Lord's favor.
>
> —Luke 4:18–19 NRSV

DANIEL ALEXANDER PAYNE was the second notable African American to receive theological education from Lutherans. While Payne did not complete an academic degree, his education significantly improved over that of Jehu Jones Jr. (see chapter 1).

Early Life

Daniel Payne was born to free parents, London and Martha Payne, in Charleston, South Carolina, on February 24, 1811. His first marriage was to Julia Faris in 1847. She died in less than a year while giving birth to a daughter. The infant died nine months later. Payne's second marriage was to Eliza Clarke in 1853. In his autobiography, Payne recalls that his grandfather, London Payne Sr., who changed the spelling of his name from Paine to Payne, was the son of an Englishman who emigrated from England to Massachusetts.[1] His grandfather served in the Revolutionary War and eventually moved his family from Massachusetts to Jamestown, Virginia. According to Daniel, the young free-born London Payne was lured into a boat, taken to Charleston, South Carolina, and sold as a slave to a house and sign painter. London worked and purchased his freedom for one thousand dollars.

Daniel writes very fondly of his father and mother. London Payne promised, "That if the Lord would give him a son, that son should be consecrated to him, and named after the Prophet Daniel."[2] He wrote in his autobiography that his parents dedicated him to God before he was born, taught him to read and write, and took him regularly to the Methodist weekly class meetings at Cumberland Street Methodist Episcopal Church, where they were members. His father died when Daniel was four years old. Daniel was separated too soon from his mother as well. Martha Payne died of consumption when he was nine. After that, Daniel was raised by his great-aunt, Sarah Bordeaux.[3] She provided for his needs and inspired him to "attain a noble character."[4] Daniel did not have to worry about necessities like many other Blacks in Charleston.

His social environment allowed him to associate with the white and Black elite, including the naturalist Lutheran churchman, Dr. John Bachman, and Thomas E. Bonneau.[5] Because of these relationships, and through the assistance of the Brown Fellowship Society of Charleston and other benefactors, Daniel studied at the Minors' Moralist Society School for Colored Children. The father of Daniel's brother-in-law was one of the wealthiest Blacks in Charleston and the co-founder of the Minors' Moralist school.[6] During the 1818/19 school term, he reports that he gained proficiency in spelling, reading, writing, and ciphering.[7] The chief books used for reading were monographs of the histories of Greece, Rome, and England; while the "Columbian Orator" was used for training in the art of speaking.[8] Payne developed an insatiable curiosity very early and lived in a context where he pursued his learning interest.

Trained early in Methodist traditions at Cumberland Methodist Church, Payne pursued a rigorous self-directed study program at Minor's Moralist Society School.[9] He studied geography and biology, mathematics and languages, pedagogy, philosophy, and theology.[10] In his autobiography, Payne displays his intellectual ambition:

> On a Thursday morning, I bought a Greek grammar, a lexicon, and a Greek Testament. On that same day I mastered the

> Greek alphabet; on Friday I learned to write them; on Saturday morning I translated the first chapter of Matthew's Gospel from Greek to English. My very soul rejoiced and exulted in the glorious triumph. Next came the Latin and the French. Meanwhile I was pushing my studies in drawing and coloring til I was able to produce a respectable flower, fruit, or animal on paper and on velvet.[11]

A book influential to Daniel's life was *John Brown's Self-Interpreting Bible*.[12] "The preface to this Bible contained a brief biographical sketch of John Brown of Haddington, Scotland. According to the sketch, Brown mastered Latin, Greek, and Hebrew without a teacher."[13] Payne might have concluded that he could do the same thing. Daniel's intellectual pursuits included a range of topics, allowing him to develop a working familiarity with several disciplines.

Adult Life

At the age of eighteen in 1829, Daniel established his own school. He taught three children during the day and three adults at night. He charged a fee of fifty cents per month per pupil. Unfortunately, however, his first school failed.[14] The monthly income generated from the school amounted to a mere three dollars, which proved insufficient to sustain him financially. In 1830 he reopened the school, and by 1835 he reported a student enrollment of sixty. His students included both free Blacks and enslaved people.[15] On April 1, 1835, the South Carolina General Assembly passed bill No. 2639: An Act to Amend the Law relating to Slaves and Free Persons of Color, which forced Payne to close his school for a second time. The law stated:

> If any free person of color or slave shall keep any school or other place of instruction for teaching any slaves or free person of color to read or write, such free person of color or slave shall be liable to . . . fine, imprisonment, and corporal punishment as are by this Act imposed and inflicted upon free persons of color for teaching slaves to read or write.[16]

The law was a reaction to slave rebellions such as those by Denmark Vesey and Nat Turner. While literacy among enslaved persons was discouraged and even prohibited by law, there were instances where some enslaved individuals managed to gain access to education and acquire reading and writing skills. Both Denmark Vesey and Nat Turner are notable examples of enslaved individuals who were literate and used their literacy to challenge the institution of slavery. White Carolinians were apprehensive about the abolitionist movement. They were alarmed by Daniel and others like him teaching free Blacks and enslaved people to read and write because they worried, they would rise against them. Payne took the closure of his school very hard. Later, when ordained a Lutheran pastor, he remarked in his ordination sermon:

> Sir, I taught school in Charleston for five years. In 1834, our state legislature enacted a law to prohibit colored teachers. My school was filled with children and youth of the most promising talents: and when I looked upon them and remembered that in a few more weeks this school shall be closed, and I be permitted no more to teach them, notwithstanding, I had been a professor seven years, I began to question the existence of the Almighty and to say, if indeed there is a God, does he deal justly? Is he a just God? Is he a holy Being? If so, why does he permit a handful of dying men thus to oppress us? Why does he permit them to hinder me from teaching these children, when nature, reason and Revelation command me to teach them? Thus I began to question the divine government and to murmur at the administration of His providence. And could I do otherwise, while slavery's cruelties were pressing and grinding my soul in the dust, and robbing me and my people of those privileges which it was hugging to its breast, and giving thousands to perpetuate the blessing which it was tearing away from us? Sir, the very man who made the law alluded to, did that very year, increase the property of South Carolina College.[17]

With the closing of his school in 1835, Daniel turned to friends including Rev. John Bachman for advice. Daniel determined to go north. With letters of recommendation from Bachman and several clergy members, Daniel sailed from Charleston on May 9, 1835, and arrived in New York City the following Wednesday. Payne delivered his letters of introduction to several people, including Lutheran pastor Daniel Strobel, who had been among the pastors who presided at the ordination of Jehu Jones Jr. Strobel attributed Daniel's arrival in his office to providence because he had been informed that the Society of Inquiry on Missions at Gettysburg, Pennsylvania, had resolved to educate a "talented, pious young man of color for the intellectual, moral, and social elevation of the free colored people of this country."[18] The Society was a Lutheran abolitionist organization that wished to support an African American for four years of study at Gettysburg Lutheran Seminary.[19] According to Nelson Strobert, the Society "took primary responsibility for financing Payne's education at Gettysburg."[20] Additionally, Payne cut wood, shined boots, and shaved people to assist with his financial needs. Payne's recollection of his discernment about seminary education includes the following encouragement from Strobel: "Now, if you will go to Gettysburg and study theology there, you will be better fitted than you are now for usefulness among your people."[21] Perhaps Strobel and the Lutherans learned from the distressing experience of Jehu Jones Jr.

Theological Education

Payne left New York ten days after his arrival to begin studies at the Gettysburg Lutheran Seminary.

Although Daniel initially did not want to embrace the doctrines of Lutheranism, he became a Lutheran while in the Lutheran academy. Payne reminisced about his dedicated period of studying Lutheran doctrines prior to his enrollment at Gettysburg Seminary.

> I spent a few days carefully examining the doctrines of the Lutheran Church, as presented in the "Unabridged Popular Theology" of Dr. Schmucker; and then I consented, being convinced that the students of divinity at Gettysburg were not screwed down to the Procrustean bedstead—that, in short, I would there be in the hands of a teacher who would be as liberal as he was Christian and learned.[22]

Image 2.1. The Lutheran Theological Seminary in 1863. Gettysburg, Pennsylvania.

Source: Civil War photographs, 1861–1865, Library of Congress, Prints and Photographs Division.

Payne's entry in his journal, which he began while a student at Gettysburg, indicates that he formally joined the Lutheran Church:

> Saturday, Ninth-September, 1835. Tomorrow I shall receive the ordinance of confirmation in the Lutheran Church and then the Lord's supper. O[h] my God, I earnestly pray thee, to prepare my heart for the enjoyment of the same. O[h] give me thy spirit.[23]

Payne's experience at Gettysburg Seminary offered at least two outstanding opportunities. First, although he was very much intent upon ordination as a Methodist early in his life, the situation at the seminary provided access to ordination. Second, Payne's academic preparation helped mold his contributions to American Christianity and education. Payne cherished his experiences at Gettysburg. He repeatedly referred to them in his writings. In the first published volume *Recollections of Seventy Years*, dedicated to the faculty, alumni, and the Society of Inquiry on Missions of the Gettysburg Seminary, he regards them as his "greatest earthly benefactors."[24] Daniel's course of study was a primary concern in his writings. He writes, "During the time I was at Gettysburg I studied German, Hebrew, Greek, ecclesiastical history, mental philosophy, archaeology, and systematic theology."[25] Daniel focused on education and his seminary studies as a key to empowerment. In addition to study, Daniel conducted a Bible class "for the colored children in the community" in space provided by Gettysburg College.[26] Payne enjoyed sharing with younger generations his acquired knowledge.

While there were enjoyable moments, Daniel Payne, the only African American student at Gettysburg Seminary, faced a different climate than his white classmates. "For all the benefits of being a student, with the opportunity to continue learning, reading, and teaching through his theological studies, one issue continued to be with him, that is to say, isolation."[27] Payne recalls this feeling:

> This day last year, I was home amidst a large circle of friends surrounded by numerous lovely pupils. But today, where am I? More than 600 miles from the place of my nativity. Among strangers, among benefactors, but not among friends in the strict sense of that word. But I look in vain for such a one here.[28]

Payne's isolation was partly due to the unique experiences shaped by the many issues of racialism that often go unnoticed by faculty and learning peers. Racialism gives rise to race-related stress, associated with difficulties in concentration, increased anxiety, depression, and other challenges experienced by minority students in predominantly white educational institutions. Payne was no exception.

At age twenty, after completing two years of study at Gettysburg, Payne had to withdraw due to a severe accident.[29] While watching the total solar eclipse of 1832 with his naked eye, he "strained the optic nerve in his left eye" and injured his vision so badly that the result was a partial loss of sight.[30] Payne never fully recovered. This would mark the end of his formal academic education.

Ordination and Pastoral Work

When Payne withdrew from the seminary, Samuel Simon Schmucker addressed the following letter to him:

> To Mr. D. A. Payne: As you are about to leave the institution in which for about two years you have been pursuing a course of study preparatory to the holy ministry, it affords me unfeigned pleasure to testify that the effect of our daily intercourse during this time has been in unwavering confidence in the integrity of your purposes and the excellency of your character, together with the conviction that the God 'who of one blood made all nations to dwell upon the face of the earth" will accompany you through life and crown with his blessing your labors in behalf of your oppressed kinsmen after the flesh. Let the precious promises of that God who hears the cries of the oppressed, and has predicted Ethiopia's enlargement, encourage you to aim at much and let a humble and habitual reliance on his aid strengthen you for its performance. That the blessing of the Divine Saviour, who has promised to be with us always, may richly abide with you, is the prayer of your friend and brother in Christ.
>
> S.S. Schmucker
> Theological Seminary, Gettysburg,
> PA. May 12, 1837[31]

Payne held Schmucker in high regard, both for his piety and for his stance on abolition. About slavery in the United States, Schmucker wrote, "All should feel that crying injustice was inflicted by our ancestors on the poor African, by reducing him to slavery, and that we become partakers of their guilt, if we protract his degradation, and delay his restoration to the unalienable rights of man."[32] Schmucker's words resonated deeply with Payne, who additionally described him as a kind instructor who, "exhibited the tenderness of a father."[33]

Schmucker's view on the institution of slavery and its impact on African American contrasted sharply with his Southern colleague, John Bachman. Bachman, who sent Daniel Payne north, wrote:

> That the negro will remain as he is unless his form is changed by an amalgamation, which latter is revolting to us. That his intellect, although underrated, is greatly inferior to that of the Caucasian, and that he is, therefore, as far as our experience goes, incapable of self-government. That he is thrown on our protection. That our defense of slavery is contained in the Holy Scriptures. That the Scriptures teach the rights and duties of masters to rule their servants with justice and kindness and enjoin the obedience of servants.[34]

Lutheran views on slavery were not uniform, mirroring the views of whites in the United States. While Payne refrained from commenting on Bachman's writings, which he must have been aware of, he was grateful to Bachman for his scientific knowledge. "He exhibited to me his herbarium and his valuable collection of insects from different parts of the world."[35] Bachman invited Payne into his home, where "He took me into his parlor and introduced me to his wife and daughters." He conversed with Bachman's family "as freely as though all were of the same color and equal rank."[36] Yet, Payne was silent about Bachman's views on slavery and the social standing of Blacks in American life, which Bachman documented in his writings.

Daniel Payne also received a letter of recommendation from Professor Charles Porterfield Krauth. Krauth wrote:

> It devolved upon me, in the providence of God, to become your teacher in the languages which the Holy Spirit employed in revealing the will of God to men. I rejoice that my efforts have been successful in preparing you to read Hebrew and Greek Scriptures. Your diligence and abilities have rendered you a good linguist in the department of Sacred Philology and convinced many who have been skeptical of the capacity

> of the colored man to achieve the intellectual victors which adorn and exalt human nature.[37]

Also, in the letter, Krauth encouraged Payne to keep studying the Holy Scriptures to obtain ordination in the Church.

> Study the Bible, then, by day and night. Read it in the original. Enlarge your knowledge of Hebrew and Greek philology. Spend a portion of every day in this employment. In this way, you can make it appear what education and study can effect in your brethren and refute the slanders of their enemies. You will thus enlarge your power of being useful to men by preaching the everlasting gospel, and become "a workman that needeth not to be ashamed, rightly dividing the word of truth."[38]

With letters of encouragement from Schmucker and Krauth, Payne left Gettysburg and consulted with Bishop Morris Brown of the African Methodist Episcopal Church in May 1837. Payne's intent was set on joining the African Methodist Episcopal Church. However, he was dissuaded from joining the AME Church by "a friend of [his]

Image 2.2. Photograph of S.S. Schmucker (1799–1873).

Source: https://commons.wikimedia.org/wiki/File:Samuel_Schmucker.jpg

father,"[39] The AME Church was still moving toward higher education for its clergy.[40] Payne's rendezvous with the AME Church was placed on hold. Payne was instead licensed by President John Lawyer, organizer of the Frankean Evangelical Lutheran Synod[41] on May 25, 1837, and was ordained two years later at Fordsboro, New York.[42] Copies of licenses are rare, but the full text of D. A. Payne's license reads:

> To all to whom these presents shall come, Greeting. Be it known that Daniel A. Payne, and late a Student of Divinity in the Theology Seminary at Gettysburg, Pennsylvania, after due examination as to his experimental knowledge of religion and branches of theological and literary acquirements and other Scriptural qualification, has this day, in pursuance to the power vested in me as President of the Franckean Synod of [the] Lu[theran] C[hurch], been received as a Licentiate of said Synod and is hereby fully licensed to preach the Gospel, to administer the Ordinances of Baptism and the Lord's Supper, and to perform all other ministerial duties. This License to remain in force until the next session of the aforesaid Synod to be held on the first Thursday in October next.[43]

The Frankean Synod's strong opposition to slavery caught the attention of Payne. The Synod's constitution forbade any slaveholder or one "who trafficked in human beings," or who advocated the system of slavery as it existed in the United States to a seat in its convention as a delegate.[44] Payne was a formidable anti-slavery advocate and found a natural, albeit temporary, home in the Frankean Synod. In an address to the Synod in 1839 in support of a synodical report to end slavery, Payne said,

> The slaves are sensible to the oppression exercised by their masters and they see these masters, on the Lord's day worshipping in his holy Sanctuary. They hear their masters professing Christianity; they see their masters preaching the gospel; they hear these masters praying in their families, and they know that oppression and slavery are inconsistent with the Christian religion; therefore they scoff at religion itself—mock their masters and distrust . . . the goodness and justice of God.

> Yes, I have known them even to question his existence. I speak not of what others have told me, but of what I have seen and heard from the slaves themselves. I have heard the mistress ring the bell for family prayer, and I have seen the servants immediately begin to sneer and laugh; and have heard them declare they would not go in to prayers; adding, if I do go in she will only just read, "Servants, obey your masters," but she will not read "break every yoke, and let the oppressed go free." I have seen colored men at the church door, scoffing at the ministers, while they were preaching, and saying, you had better go home, and set your slaves free. A few nights ago, between 10 and 11 o'clock a runaway slave came to the house when I live for safety and succor. I asked him if he was a Christian, "no sir," he said, "white men treat us so bad in Mississippi that we can't be Christians."[45]

A soft-spoken speaker, Payne used fiery imagery in concluding his address to the Frankeans. Payne's "Slavery Brutalizes Man" address is seen as a critical factor in the Frankean Synod's decision to accept and publish the report to end slavery and as a defining moment in the life of this remarkable pastor and educational leader. Payne's speech to the Franckean Synod rivals the "I Have a Dream" sermon so readily identified with Martin Luther King Jr. and the movement for African American civil rights. However, unlike King's "Dream" sermon, Payne's "Slavery Brutalizes Man" is largely unknown to the masses.

Many Lutherans condemned the Frankeans for their indifference to the Lutheran Confessions. Anti-Frankeans criticized the church body for taking a high moral path in resistance to slavery by forfeiting Lutheran identity. Frankean abolitionism is discounted as an un-Lutheran adaptation to antebellum revivalism and reform. At the same time, the positions of most Lutherans on slavery oscillated from quietism to apologies parading as neutralism, which did not raise the identity question.

Following ordination, the Frankean Synod did not have a congregational ministry assignment for Payne.[46] Payne offered himself to the Frankeans as a missionary to the West Indies, but the Synod could not secure the funds to effect a call.[47] With no assignment in the Lutheran Church, at 26 years old, Payne assumed the pastorate of Liberty Street Presbyterian Church, a Black congregation in East Troy, New York, near Albany. [48] He went to the Presbyterian congregation with permission of the Frankean Synod president, John Lawyer.[49] Payne was followed as pastor of Liberty Street Presbyterian Church by Henry Highland Garnet, an American abolitionist, minister, educator, and orator. Garnet was pastor of Liberty Church from 1840 to 1848.[50]

After assuming his duties with the Presbyterians, Payne was asked to represent the community at a National Moral Reform Society meeting, an abolitionist group. Abolitionist Lewis Tappan and other members of the executive committee of the Anti-Slavery Society were present. The group invited Payne to serve as one of its public lecturers "with a salary of $300 per year and traveling expenses."[51] He turned

Image 2.3. The Bishop's Council of 1892, Philadelphia, PA. Daniel Payne is seated on the first row with his hands folded in his lap.

Source: Schomburg Center for Research in Black Culture, Manuscripts, Archives and Rare Books Division. Courtesy of the New York Public Library Digital Collections. Public Domain.

down the offer. Payne wrote, "But I had consecrated myself to the pulpit and the work of salvation. Could I turn aside for so high a position and so holy a calling?"[52] Payne would back up this commitment to ministry by serving for over fifty years as a pastor, educator, and bishop.

At the end of a two-year pastorate at Liberty Street Presbyterian Church in East Troy, with no Lutheran calls to a ministry pending, Payne moved to Philadelphia. In Philadelphia, Payne writes that he was "in daily association with the leaders,"[53] including Bishop Morris Brown, pastor of the AME Church in Charleston. In 1822, Brown and the entire AME Church, and other Black churches were banned from the State of South Carolina. This decision was based on allegations made by white individuals, who claimed that members of the AME Church were involved in the Denmark Vesey rebellion.[54] While Payne did not know Brown while the two were in Charleston, Bishop Brown is credited with bringing Payne into the AME Church because of their relationship formed in Philadelphia.[55] He joined Bethel African Methodist Episcopal Church in 1842.[56] That same year he was admitted to the Philadelphia Annual Conference of the AME Church. He was transferred to the Baltimore Conference and was named the pastor of Bethel Church, Baltimore, in 1845. The General Conference of 1848 appointed Payne to write the history of the AME Church.[57] In 1852, ten years after becoming a member of the African Methodist Episcopal Church, Payne was elected the sixth bishop of that church. He served forty-one years as a bishop and twenty years as senior bishop.

In 1852, the Cincinnati Conference of the Methodist Episcopal Church invited Bishop Payne to represent the AME Church in initial conversations about plans to open a school of college grade at Xenia, Ohio.[58] The school was organized and constituted a corporate body named Wilberforce University in April 1852.[59] The Methodist Episcopal Church operated the college until 1862 when the Civil War divided the chief patrons of the schools.[60] Payne purchased the school for the AME Church on the March, 10 1863, for ten thousand dollars. On July 3, 1863, Wilberforce University was reopened as an African Methodist Episcopal Church institution. Payne was named president and became the first African American college president in the United States. He served thirteen years as president; from 1863 to 1876; Payne died at 82 on November 2, 1893.

Legacy

Image 2.4. Pennsylvania Historical and Museum Commission historical marker, 1991.

On March 10, 1991, the Pennsylvania Historical and Museum Commission with Gettysburg College, a college of the Evangelical Lutheran Church in America, and the Lutheran Theological Seminary dedicated a state historical marker in honor of Bishop Daniel Alexander Payne at 239 N. Washington Street, Gettysburg, Pennsylvania.

On February 16, 2011, Gettysburg Seminary celebrated the bicentenary of the birth of Daniel Alexander Payne. Michael Cooper-White, president of Gettysburg Seminary, said, "This giant of the Church in the

19th century established a legacy unsurpassed by any other Gettysburg Seminary alumnus/a as he served as pastor and AME bishop, as well as founding president of Wilberforce University in Ohio."[61]

Many in the AME Church consider Payne the intellectual leader of that body during his long years of service. He was the first bishop to have a formal theological education, although his school days were few. Harry L. Dox, one of the leaders of the Frankean Synod, commented lamentably about Payne and the Frankean Lutheran Synod, "He left it, not because he did not love it. He left it because it had no place for him. Because he felt that he had no right to expect cooperation from the denomination at large in any movement he might make on behalf of colored people."[62] Daniel Payne would have been a strong leader in any denomination. His exit was a profound loss for Lutherans in the United States. There is little curiosity about why Daniel Payne left the Frankean Synod. The Frankeans welcomed Daniel but were unprepared to integrate him into the church's life entirely. They did not seem to understand their full responsibility to Daniel Payne. The Frankeans did not sense the unique needs and missional realities buzzing in Payne's head. Like Jehu Jones Jr., he was a Black man in a white denomination that was not yet ready to include him fully. In official documents, the Frankeans were quite willing to live by Christ's law of love, but that was as far as it went. They were not willing to provide significant financial aid to Daniel Payne in his efforts to plant a congregation. While the Frankeans opposed slavery, Daniel Payne's calling to work with Black communities never took center stage. Daniel Payne was the second African American to be ordained as a Lutheran pastor in the United States.

Notes

1. Daniel A. Payne, *Recollections of Seventy Years* (New York: Arno Press, 1969), 11–12.
2. Payne, *Recollections of Seventy Years,* 16.
3. Legerton, *Historic Churches of Charleston,* 13.
4. Paul R. Griffin, *Black Theology as the Foundation of Three Methodist Colleges: The Educational Views and Labors of Daniel Payne, Joseph Price and Isaac Lane* (Lanham, MD: University Press of America, 1984), 96.
5. Griffin, *Black Theology as the Foundation of Three Methodist Colleges,* 96.

6. Griffin, *Black Theology as the Foundation of Three Methodist Colleges*, 96.
7. Griffin, *Black Theology as the Foundation of Three Methodist Colleges*, 15.
8. First appearing in 1797, *The Columbian Orator*, a collection of political essays, poems, and dialogues, was widely used in American schoolrooms in the first quarter of the nineteenth century to teach reading and speaking. Many of the speeches included in the anthology celebrated "republican" virtues and promoted patriotism, and this was typical of many readers of that period. The *Columbian Orator* is an example of progymnasmata, containing examples for students to copy and imitate (19th Century Schoolbooks Collection, Digital Research Library, University of Pittsburgh.)

   The Columbian Orator, became a symbol not only of human rights, but also of the power of eloquence and articulation.
9. Payne, *Recollections of Seventy Years*, 11–12.
10. Payne, *Recollections of Seventy Years*, 2. Payne patterned his early learning after the life of the Reverend John Brown of Haddington, Scotland. Brown was the author of what was called the "Self-Interpreting Bible." According to Payne, Brown was a self-educated person who learned Latin, Greek, and Hebrew. He determined that if Brown could learn "without a living teacher" so could he. From the age of thirteen, Payne began to teach himself in such areas as botany, geography, natural philosophy, chemistry, and astronomy.
11. Payne, *Recollections of Seventy Years*, 22–23.
12. Charles D. Killian, *Bishop Daniel A. Payne: Black Spokesman for Reform* (PhD diss., Indiana University), 1971, 4
13. Henry J. Young, *Major Black Religious Leaders: 1755–1940* (Nashville: Parthenon Press, 1977), 61.
14. Young, *Major Black Religious Leaders*, 19.
15. Young, *Major Black Religious Leaders*, 62.
16. Payne, *Recollections of Seventy Years*, 27.
17. Daniel A Payne, "Slavery Brutalizes Man," 1839. In June 1839, Payne delivered a speech at Fordsboro, New York, on the occasion of his ordination by the Franckean Synod of the Lutheran Church. Payne's speech appeared in the Lutheran Herald and Journal of Fort Plain, NY, Franckean Synod 1:15 (August 1, 1839), 113–14. A copy of it is available at Lutheran Theological Seminary, Abdel Ross Wentz Library, Gettysburg, Pennsylvania.
18. Payne, *Recollections of Seventy Years*, 44.
19. Nelson T. Strobert, *Daniel Alexander Payne: The Venerable Preceptor of the African Methodist Episcopal Church* (Lanham: University Press of America, 2012), 16.
20. Strobert, *Daniel Alexander Payne*, 16.

21. Payne, *Recollections of Seventy Years*, 44
22. Payne, *Recollections of Seventy Years*, 45.
23. Journal of Daniel A. Payne. The text of the unpublished journal appears in Josephus Coan, *Daniel Alexander Payne: Christian Educator* (Philadelphia, PA: AME Book Concern, 1935), 47.
24. Daniel Payne, *The Semi-Centenary and the Retrospection of the African Methodist Episcopal Church* (New York, Books for Libraries, reprint, 1972).
25. Payne, *Recollections of Seventy Years*, 59.
26. On motion of J. F. McFarland & D. Gilbert Resolved that Mr. Payne a Col'd Theological student be permitted to meet his bible class of Col'd people in one of the rooms of the College. Gettysburg College, Trustee Minutes Book, 1837, p. 39.
27. Strobert, *Daniel Alexander Payne*, 19.
28. Strobert, *Daniel Alexander Payne*, 19
29. Strobert, *Daniel Alexander Payne*, 60.
30. T.W. Lynn, *The Total Solar Eclipse of 1832, July 27.* The Observatory, Vol. 24, p. 386–386 (1901) "The eclipse was observed in the afternoon as a partial one by Gambart at Marseilles (*Ast. Nach* * No. 232, vol. x. col. 259), by Santini at Padua, by messrs. Johnson and Armstrong at St. Helena, and by Don Sanchez Cerquero and Don Saturnio Montojo at San Ferando (*Memoirs of R.A.S.* vol vi. P. 191)." p. 386.
31. Payne, *Recollections of Seventy Years*, 63.
32. Samuel Simon Schmucker. Elements of Popular Theology with Special References to the Doctrins of the Reformation, as Avowed before the Diet of Augsburg in MDXXX (1st ed: Andover: Gould and Newman, 1834, 252.
33. Payne, *Recollections of Seventy Years*, 59
34. A.H. Malthy, *The Southern Apostasy*, The New Englander, New Haven, F.W. Northrop, Vol.12.1854, 642–643.
35. Payne, *Recollections of Seventy Years*, 24.
36. Payne, *Recollections of Seventy Years*, 24
37. Payne, *Recollections of Seventy Years*, 63.
38. Payne, *Recollections of Seventy Years*, 63–64.
39. Payne, *Recollections of Seventy Years*, 64.
40. Payne, *Recollections of Seventy Years*, 64.
41. Todd W. Nichol, *All These Lutherans* (Minneapolis: Augsburg Publishers, 1986). The Frankean Synod was a Lutheran church body in the United States in the 19th century. The Synod was formed on 25 May 1837 by four Lutheran clergyman and twenty-seven lay delegates in New York who were dissatisfied with the Hartwick Synod's position on slavery. The

Synod was named in memory of the Pietist cleric and humanitarian of the Foundation at the University of Halle, August Hermann Francke (1863–1727). The abolitionist convictions of the Frankean Synod were embedded in the main body of its constitution. No minister who was a slaveholder or engaged in the traffic of human beings or advocated the system of slavery then existing in the United States could be accepted into the synod nor could a layperson practicing any of the above serve as a delegate to synodical meetings. By 1848 these restrictions were increased to include laity who "justified the sin of slavery" and clergy "who did not oppose" it. The Frankean Synod was strongly abolitionist, pro-temperance, and pacifist.

42. Minutes, Franckean Synod, 1838, 27; 1839, 17; 1840, 32.
43. Minutes, Franckean Synod, 1838, 27; 1839, 17; 1840, 32.
44. Minutes, Frankean Synod, May 1837, 18.
45. Excerpt from address: "*Speech by Brother Daniel A. Payne*" delivered at the Frankean Synod, June 1, 1839, in *Lutheran Herald*, Aug. 1, 1839, pp. 113–14. An account of his ordination by the Franckean is written in the same publication, 152.
46. The record is unclear regarding what financial transactions occurred between Payne and the Franckean Synod, but at the time of his transfer Payne wrote a letter requesting a "dismissal" to the "Colored Methodist Church." "The Synod however refused to grant the request 'until he had discharged our claims and that he should be honorably dismissed.' "A letter was directed to refund the amount due from him to this Synod but apparently nothing came of it, and after 1846 his name was dropped from the clerical roll of the Synod." Quoted from Kreider, *History of the United Lutheran Synod of New York and New England*, 153.
47. Douglas C. Strange. "Bishop Daniel Payne and the Lutheran Church." *Lutheran Quarterly*, 16 (no. 4), November 1965, p. 358.
48. Harry Bradshaw Matthews. *African American Freedom Journey in New York and Related Sites, 1823–1870: Freedom Knows no Color* (Africana Homestead Legacy Publishers, 2008), 12. The location (Troy) was not far from the Northern end of the Susquehanna River at Cooperstown, well within the territorial range of the Franckean Synod, inclusive of the countries of Chenango, Otsego, Schoharie, and Rensselaer.
49. Minutes, *Frankean Synod*, 27.
50. Henry Highland Garnet. *Let Slavery Die: The Life of Henry Highland Garnet and His 1865 Discourse Before the House of Representatives* (Log Cottage Press, 1865).
51. Payne, *Recollections of Seventy Years*, 60.
52. Payne, *Recollections of Seventy Years*, 67.

53. Payne, *Recollections of Seventy Years*, 67.
54. Maurie McInnis. "The First Attack on Charleston's AME Church." June 19, 2015. https://slate.com/news-and-politics/2015/06/charleston-shooting-the-attack-on-the-ame-church-is-rooted-in-the-citys-vicious-history-of-racial-fears-and-violence.html
55. Payne, *Recollections of Seventy Years*, 73–74.
56. Thomas R. Noon. "Daniel Payne and the Lutherans." *Concordia Historical Institute Quarterly*. 50.2 (Summer 1977): 51–69.
57. Daniel A. Payne and Charles Spencer. *History of the African Methodist Episcopal Church* (New York: Johnson Reprint Corporation, 1968).
58. James T. Campbell. *Songs of Zion: The African Methodist Episcopal Church in the United States and South Africa*. The University of North Carolina Press 1998, 263.
59. Fredrick A. McGinnis. *A History and Interpretation of Wilberforce University* (Blanchester, Ohio: Brown Publishing, 1941), 29–37.
60. McGinnis. *A History and Interpretation of Wilberforce University*, 37
61. *Gettysburg Seminary and AME Leaders to Mark Bicentennial of Daniel Alexander Payne in Worship Event Feb 16th*. www.ltsg.edu/LTSG-News/February-2011/Gettysburg-Seminary-and-AME-Leaders-to-Mark-Bicent. Retrieved November 6, 2011.
62. Strange, "Bishop Daniel Payne and the Lutheran Church," 359.

CHAPTER 3

Boston Jenkins Drayton

The First Ordained African American Lutheran in South Carolina

Image 3.1. Portrait of Boston Jenkins Drayton. Illustration from *Cases decided in the Supreme Court of the Republic of Liberia between 1850 and 1907.*

Source: https://babel.hathitrust.org/cgi/pt?id=mdp.35112102858059&view=1up&seq=9

Boston Jenkins Drayton (1821–1865) exercised care and provided hope, direction, and concern for people still held in bondage. He was influential in the community as a leader and was the first African American ordained in South Carolina by Lutherans. Erskine Clarke writes about Drayton and others like him: "They were the leaders of their people, providing some relief from the cruel realities of slavery."[1] Despite being viewed with uneasiness by the white community, Drayton and other black leaders in the church had considerable influence among free and enslaved Blacks.

Early Life and Mission Work

Boston Jenkins Drayton was born in Charleston, South Carolina, in 1821. Like Jehu Jones Jr. and Daniel A. Payne, the Reverend John Bachman of St. John's Lutheran Church, Charleston influenced Drayton to seek ordination as a Lutheran minister. Bachman found Drayton "[A] pious and talented person with more education than most of the Negro members of St. John's."[2] Drayton's education proved invaluable in his role at St. John's and in subsequent roles of increasing responsibility, where he consistently demonstrated strong leadership skills and managed large numbers of people.

For several years, Drayton served as one of the African American lay assistants serving the "colored" congregation at St. John's.[3] While at St. John's, he was valued for his role in supporting order and moral self-restraint among Black church members. However, Drayton and other Black leaders in the church were regarded with distrust because they were influential among people who should be controlled exclusively by their masters. They spoke with authority among people who should have no influence. They held the allegiance of people who should have no fidelity except to masters and mistresses. Drayton and other Black leaders in Charleston determined they could not remain in the city because of the mistrust and the evil character of slave culture. In 1845 Drayton contacted the Reverend John Christian Hope, president of the South Carolina Synod (Lutheran Church), and announced his "intention to go to Liberia as a missionary."[4] Having knowledge of the American Colonization Society's efforts initiated in his attention towards Africa. The American Colonization Society had laid the groundwork for establishing a colony in Africa specifically intended for free Blacks and formerly enslaved individuals. Society members believed Blacks and whites could not live freely together in the United States.[5] The organization served as a conduit through which several thousand free Blacks and formerly enslaved people passed from life in the United

States to a complicated future in Liberia. Many free Blacks criticized the society's mission.[6] However, others like Drayton volunteered to relocate to Liberia. Drayton hoped to serve as a missionary to Black settlers in Liberia.

Synod President Hope scheduled Drayton's departure for Africa before the synod convention.[7] The minutes of the General Synod indicate that persons of African descent primarily supported Drayton's missionary work: "How far of this mission, voluntarily undertaken by an individual, and supported, in a great measure, by the people of his own color, will be productive of good, must be left to Him who is the ruler of nations, and who is able to convert the most untoward events into instruments of great and abiding mercy."[8] While the South Carolina Synod offered hope and prayers that Drayton's mission would succeed, the Synod offered no financial support until the mission proved to be successful. The Synod wrote, "It is to be hoped that this self-denying brother will share largely in the prayers and sympathies of the church, and we would recommend that our Missionary Society (if his mission is likely to be successful) should extend to him some pecuniary aid."[9] By not giving him money for support, the Synod Missionary Fund expressed no tangible optimism that Drayton's mission would succeed. Though the South Carolina Synod was not impressed enough with Drayton's proposed mission to support him financially or otherwise, he had a supporting ear in Baltimore. The Reverend Benjamin Kurtz wrote, "We feel confident that this movement of our South Carolina brethren will be viewed with satisfaction by the whole church, and we trust that they will go forward and build up and sustain a mission that will do for Africa what Schwartz, and Zigenbarg [sic] and our German and Danish missionaries did for India, and what we trust br. Heyer and Gunn will do for the Teloogoos."[10] However, there was no record of a contribution attached to Reverend Kurtz's encouraging words either.

Boston Drayton was the first African American ordained in South Carolina by Lutherans. He was a missionary in Cap Palmas in the newly formed Republic of Maryland. The Republic of Maryland was created in 1831 by the Maryland State Legislature to ship free Blacks and emancipated slaves from the United States to Africa.[11] In December 1831, the Maryland State Legislature allocated ten thousand dollars for twenty-six years to transport ten thousand free Blacks and formerly enslaved people from the United States and four hundred enslaved people from the Caribbean islands to Africa. The Maryland State Legislature also organized the Maryland State Colonization Society as a branch of the American Colonization Society, which founded the colony of Liberia at Monrovia on January 7, 1822.[12] Members of the organization believed that free Blacks and emancipated slaves could not be integrated into white America and should live in Africa. Drayton signed on to the Maryland State Colonization Society's desire to promote "temporal happiness" among free persons of color and "be the means of spreading the light of civilization and the Gospel in Africa."[13] Drayton may have accepted without question the view of the Maryland State Colonization Society that a "backward pagan" Africa was a place where Blacks would have opportunities to demonstrate their talents without interference from whites. In 1834 a settler community of free Blacks and ex-slaves was established, with Cape Palmas as its center. Boston Drayton participated in the Colonization Society's transfer of freeborn Blacks and emancipated slaves by sailing to West Africa

Drayton issued a report to South Carolina Lutherans on his first days as a missionary:

> I have been blessed by the Lord to find a field of labor not in competition with any others, that the Lord has reserved for us. The Governor has told me that I can have as much land as I want to build on, in the name of the Lutheran Church in America. I will begin a school. Already I have about thirty children engaged and five or ten native boys. The schoolhouse will cost about $800, because lumber is hard to get. I will build it large enough that it may be use as a church. We shall call it the "Lutheran Missionary School."[14]

Boston Drayton served as a Lutheran missionary in Cape Palmas for one year. Drayton's work, although short-lived, was the first missionary activity on the African Continent by Lutherans in North America. Histories of Lutheran mission work in Africa refer to the Reverend Morris Officer as the first American Lutheran to commence mission work there. Officer sailed from New York City on the *Martha Clark* to Liberia in December 1852 and began work at Kaw Mendi.[15] Drayton was in Africa six years before Officer sailed. Drayton was twenty-four years old when he started his vocation.

Ordination

Drayton's ordination came ten years after Daniel Payne's and thirteen years after the ordination of Jehu Jones Jr. These ordinations are testimony to the presence of Blacks in St. John's Lutheran Church, Charleston, for an extended period. The ordination of Boston Drayton is also an indication that Bachman evolved to a point where he felt he could have Blacks ordained in South Carolina rather than in the North.

John Bachman maintained two contrasting views of African Americans. On the one hand, he encouraged and sent three able African Americans into ministry in the Lutheran Church. At the same time, he argued that Africans could not be made equal with their white masters. In 1857 Bachman wrote a letter to *The Lutheran Missionary* after they published a piece against slavery. The newspaper was in Pittsburg, run by William Passavant, who opposed slavery, making him an outlier in the North as few Lutherans outside the Frankean Synod were radical abolitionists. Passavant framed his opposition partly by three resolutions presented to the Evangelical Lutheran General Synod convened in Lancaster at Trinity Lutheran Church from May 1 to May 8, 1862. The Lutherans also presented the resolutions to President Abraham Lincoln. The resolutions, published May 15, 1862, were cuttingly critical of slavery as it existed in the South. In his letter to the newspaper, Bachman protested the inclusion of the resolutions, writing, "Whilst we implicitly receive the Scriptural doctrine of the unity of the human race, we are not blind to the fact of the wide difference in some of the verities of men, the physical form, the color, and the inferiority in intellect of the African tribes now in a state of mild servitude in our Southern country, were marked in them by their Creator."[16] In Bachman's racial hierarchy, people of European descent are at the top; Africans are at, or near, the bottom.

John Bachman did not arrive at his views on Blacks and slavery after he arrived in South Carolina. Born in a village in the Hudson Valley in New York, John Bachman did not question slavery, at least not on record. Slavery was legal in New York while Bachman matured. In 1799 New York State passed a Gradual Emancipation Act that freed slave children born after July 1799, but allowed slavery to continue until 1828. Bachman's father, a farmer, owned several enslaved people.

In the move from the North to South Carolina, Bachman would see and experience slavery writ large. He never uttered a word about whether slavery surprised him or not. However, he believed slavery was part of the natural order and defended this belief in many of his writings. Worth noting is the presence of a stone memorial plaque in the chapel of Ebenezer Lutheran Church, Columbia, South Carolina, honoring William Kunhardt Bachman, son of Rev. John Bachman. William was a vestryman at Ebenezer for over forty years and was recognized by the congregation for "Bearing arms for his State and the Confederacy."

After serving a year as a Lutheran missionary in Maryland, West Africa, in 1846 Drayton sailed from Monrovia to New York. While Drayton made his Christian and spiritual home among Lutherans most of his adult life, when he traveled to the United States in 1846, he separated from Lutheranism. No letter of resignation exists, but what is clear is that Lutherans did not support Drayton's work. In 1847, he was baptized a Baptist by the pastor of First African Baptist Church, the Reverend Robert Ryland, in Richmond, Virginia. He was appointed by the Foreign Missionary Board (Southern Baptist Church) in January 1848, arriving in Liberia via the *Amazon* in the Spring of 1848.[17] The Baptist Foreign Mission Board listed Drayton as a missionary from 1848 to 1865. In a doctoral dissertation written at Southeastern Baptist Theological Seminary in 2008, Thomas Alexander Kinchen, former president of the Baptist College of Florida, described Boston Drayton's work in Maryland and Liberia.[18] Drayton preached at Providence Church, founded by Lott Carey in 1822 in Cape Palmas. He served as Superintendent of Baptist Missions in West Africa. He married the daughter of Rev. James Edens, pastor at First Presbyterian Church in Monrovia. No record of Drayton's resignation from the Lutheran ministry exists.

Political Life

Drayton subsequently pursued a career in politics. He served as Lieutenant Governor of Maryland, West Africa under Governor William P. Prout in 1856. The Free State of Maryland had a population of fewer than one thousand settlers, primarily from the US state of Maryland. The settlers included freeborn Blacks and a mixture of domestic and manumitted field-hand former slaves. They would now govern and rule over twenty thousand disenfranchised Africans. Prout managed to keep office for eighteen months, but then citizens grew restive because there was no marked improvement in their lives. The Grebo, an ethnic subgroup within the larger Kru group in Maryland, resisted the Maryland colonists' efforts to control their trade in enslaved people and other goods.[19] In December 1855, Drayton led a coup and overthrew Prout from office. Drayton was elected Governor of Maryland unanimously in April 1856, serving as the final governor from 1856 to 1857. By December of 1856, relations between the US Black settlers and the native Grebo and Kru populations had deteriorated into open warfare, which began during Drayton's term as governor. Historians John Hazlehurst and Boneval Latrobe fault Boston Drayton for the Grebo and Kru wars:

> It was under his administration that the native war began. Without the cautious and sagacious and patient temper of his predecessors, Governor Drayton's course has been said to have brought on a conflict resulting in many deaths on both sides.[20]

With a war raging, Drayton petitioned the Liberian government for support. In response, Liberian President J. J. Roberts sent a force of Liberian settlers and a joint military campaign by the two groups of African American colonists put down the Grebo rebellion. Drayton and his government recognized that the Republic of Maryland could not survive as an independent state. Following a referendum in 1857, Drayton led Maryland in joining Liberia as Maryland County. Drayton stepped down as governor on March 18, 1857.

In 1861 Boston Drayton, whose education background did not include Law, was appointed the third Chief Justice of Liberia's Supreme Court by President Stephen Allen Benson. Drayton's early education in Charleston, his leadership at St. John's Lutheran Church, and his experience as a missionary and colonial governor were the extent of his preparation for the high office. He served as Chief Justice until 1864. Boston Jenkins Drayton died on December 12, 1864, from a canoeing accident in the Poor River near Grand Cess, Liberia.

Boston Drayton and Lutheranism

Boston Drayton represents a squandered opportunity for a Lutheran presence among Blacks in the United States and Africa. After arriving in Cape Palmas, West Africa, Drayton diligently began planting a Lutheran mission congregation. Drayton received land grants from the government of Maryland and enrolled children in a school. Drayton intended to build a missionary school in the name of the Lutheran Church in the United States. Had Drayton succeeded, Lutherans would have been among the first denominations to establish a school in West Africa. Without the help of U.S. Lutherans, Drayton could not serve the Lutheran missionary enterprise. In the meantime, Drayton turned to the Baptists after one disappointing year as the first Lutheran missionary in Africa from the United States. With extraordinary resilience, and sheer will and determination, Drayton moved on. A member of the ruling elite, Drayton worked as a Baptist missionary while assisting in nation-building. With no college education, he followed his passion for ministry as a missionary and civil servant. Drayton served as missionary, pastor, governor, and chief justice of the Liberian Supreme Court.

Lutherans were present at the beginning of the Liberian Christian church. However, unlike Baptists, Methodists, and Episcopalians, Lutherans were not ready to support or trust the work of sharing God's word to a Black man.

Notes

1. Erskine Clark, *Wrestlin' Jacob: A Portrait of Religion in Antebellum Georgia and the Georgia and Carolina low country* (Tuscaloosa: The University of Alabama Press, 2000), 124.
2. *A History of the Lutheran Church in South Carolina*. Columbia, SC, R. L. Bryan Company. Published by The South Carolina Synod of the Lutheran Church in America. Prepared and edited by the History of Synod Committee, 1971, 272.
3. Paul P. Kuenning, *The Rise and Fall of American Lutheran Pietism: The Rejection of an Activist Heritage*. (Macon, GA: Mercer University Press, 1988).
4. *A History of The Lutheran Church in South Carolina*, 272.

5. Eric Burin, *Slavery and the Peculiar Solution: A History of the American Colonization Society*. Southern Dissent (University Press of Florida, 2008).
6. Ousmane Power-Greene, *Against Wind and Tide: The African American Struggle against the Colonization Movement* (New York, NYU Press, 2014).
7. A History of The Lutheran Church in South Carolina, 272.
8. *Minutes, General Synod*, 1845, 8–9.
9. *Minutes, General Synod*, 1845, 15.
10. *Lutheran Observer*, 13, no. 10 (October 31, 1845).
11. *The African Repository*, 14: 42. Retrieved September 21, 2022.
12. John Hazlehurst and Boneval Latrobe, *Maryland in Liberia: A History of the Colony Planted by the Maryland State Colonization Society under the auspices of the State of Maryland, U.S. at Cape Palmas on the South-West Coast of Africa, 1933–1853*. (Baltimore, MD: Peabody Publication Fund, 1885), 14–22.
13. Hazlehurst and Latrobe, *Maryland in Liberia*, 21
14. *Lutheran Observer*, 13, no. 32 (April 3, 1846).
15. Alex. J. Imhoff, *The Life of Rev. Morris Officer* (HardPress Publishing, 2012), 82–107.
16. John Bachman, Charleston, SC, November 24,1857, published in *The Missionary*, December 10, 1857, quoted from Robert Fortenbaugh, "The Representative Lutheran Periodical Press," 167.
17. This copy of a letter from Foreign Mission Board executive leader James B. Taylor informs Boston Jenkins Drayton of his missionary appointment. https://www.imb.org/175/decades/1840s/. Retrieved March 6, 2023.
18. Thomas Alenander Kinchen, *"Africa is doubtless to be evangelized": Assessing Southern Baptist Mission Focus, Education, and Spiritual Awakening Among Liberians, 1846–1880, through an examination of the ministries of John Day, John H. Cheeseman, and Boston J. Drayton*. Dissertation, Southeastern Baptist Theological Seminary, Wakeforest, NC, 2008.
19. "The Kru." *Historic Liberia*. http://historicliberia.org/the-kru/. Retrieved September 21, 2022.
20. Hazlehurst and Latrobe, *Maryland in Liberia*, 83.

CHAPTER 4

Rosa J. Young

The First Confirmed Lutheran Teacher and Mission Worker in Alabama

Image 4.1. Rosa J. Young, 1927, St. Louis, MO, Concordia House Print.

The establishment of mission congregations and weekday schools in central Alabama by the Lutheran Synodical Conference of North America resulted in a Lutheran College for African Americans at Selma, Alabama. Rosa J. Young's work and her invitation to Lutherans to share in her educational efforts in rural Alabama are an essential part of the history of higher education in America. In 1916, following the appeal of an African American woman from Rosebud, Alabama, the Lutheran Synodical Conference of North America began mission work in Central Alabama. Rosa J. Young, a public and private school teacher, wrote to Dr. Booker T. Washington at the Tuskegee Institute. In her letter, Rosa asked Washington for the names of individuals, or an association, in the

North that might help keep open the Rosebud Literary and Industrial School, which she had established in 1912. Rosa's tireless efforts on behalf of the children of Rosebud are an inseparable part of the founding of a Lutheran college at Selma, Alabama, in 1922. Rosa's story provides insight into the difficulty African Americans had obtaining higher education in that period, particularly women. Her story illuminates issues such as the poor preparation of Black teachers, the financial struggles, the effects of poverty, racism, classism, and patriarchy, and provides a view of rural Black life in the early 1900s.

Education

Following in the footsteps of predecessors Daniel Payne and Boston Drayton, Rosa embarked on her spiritual journey as a Methodist. Born May 14, 1890, in Rosebud, Alabama, she was the daughter of farmers Grant and Nancy Young. Like so much of Alabama, farming was the prevailing occupation of Wilcox County until well into the twentieth century. Grant was an ordained minister in the African Methodist Episcopal Church. Rosa was the fourth of ten children born to the Youngs. In her autobiography, *Light in the Dark Belt*, Rosa provides details about her parents Grant and Nancy Young. She is either silent about her nine siblings, or perhaps they were edited out of the story. At an early age, she decided she wanted to be a schoolteacher. She recalls, "As long as I can remember I would tell all who asked me that I was going to be a teacher."[1]

Rosa's formal education began with her attendance at a primary school run by Bruce Hines. In this school, she was introduced to the *Patterson Speller.*[2] She attended another primary school conducted at night under the tutelage of Mitchell Young, her uncle, who was a student at Tuskegee Institute. However, before her years of schooling, Rosa also received homeschooling from her mother, Nancy, who taught her children to recite the Lord's Prayer and other exercises. After briefly attending primary school, Rosa did not enroll in formal learning for several years. She writes, "The next account that I can give of myself after having lost sight of Mitchell Young was that I had no teacher."[3] In 1901, Rosa entered a school run by Professor D. L. House. House tested Rosa and placed her in the fifth grade. The instructional materials in this school included *Webster* and *Patterson* spellers and the Bible.

After completing elementary school, Rosa's parents allowed her to enroll at Payne University in Selma, Alabama. The school, founded in 1880, was named for Bishop Daniel A. Payne and affiliated with the African Methodist Episcopal Church.[4] With few financial resources, Payne offered a program of study. While identified as a "university," the institution was like a school with elementary and high school departments. Most graduates entered the teaching profession after graduating from the program.

In the fall of 1903, Grant Young accompanied his daughter to Selma, Alabama. Rosa remembers she enrolled with two hundred other students at Payne. The student body at Payne was primarily from Selma, and since Rosa was not "they laughed, jeered, mocked, and derided me because I came from the country."[5] Rosa believed she was the only student from rural Alabama, and she stood out. Life was not easy during the first two weeks. After an examination, she received a promotion to the seventh grade. Her progress went well until her parents called her home two months before the end of the school year to help with farm work. This would happen each year during her studies at Payne.

At Payne, Rosa was elected president of the Allen League, the Loyal Temperance League, and the Payne Literary Society in the second term. In her third year, as she entered the teacher education program, she found the schoolwork challenging: "In the first place, there was a new crop of teachers, and they took nothing for granted; a student had to pass or repeat the work." In 1905, Rosa accepted a summer teaching position in a school run by a Rosebud Methodist church. Rosa's income from teaching enabled her to buy everything necessary for school, including railroad fare to Selma. Funds were also available for the first month's boarding from the summer work.[6]

During the 1906/07 school term, Rosa, at age 15, served as editor of the monthly school paper, *The Payne Sentinel*. She writes, "The President also appointed me subteacher for the university."[7] She began to study for the Alabama State Teacher's Examination. Rosa passed an examination in December 1906 and taught at a public school in Oleo, Alabama. She was only in the eleventh grade. While Rosa was in her junior year at Payne, she won two prizes: a gold medal in an oratorical contest and a five-dollar award in a mathematical competition.

Rosa's final year at Payne, 1908/09, was her sixth year. She suffered the first of several nervous breakdowns that year. Rosa managed multiple challenges. Teased for her country ways by Selma's Black students, she pressed on. At Payne, Rosa assisted in publishing a newsletter. She served as a leader of student organizations, a competitor in oratorical contests, and worked as a sub-teacher, returning home yearly to help with farming. Black children were often removed from school because their hands were needed on the farm. Black children had to work alongside their parents to plant and harvest crops. She was challenging the norms of the times. The challenges, no doubt, placed tremendous pressure on her. Even with these extra demands, the faculty of Payne chose Rosa as valedictorian of her graduating class in 1909. In her commencement speech, she encouraged her classmates to leave the university "in the spirit of service, with a determination to do all in our power to uplift humanity."[8] Rosa gave her valedictorian speech while seated because she was so nervous.

Teaching Experience

Following graduation, Rosa Young left Selma for home on June 2, 1909. She was ready to fulfill her childhood dream of teaching. Black women like Rosa, who were college graduates, did not have many career paths opened to them. Yet, Rosa demonstrated a commitment to public life. While unrepresented and unable to access the educational agencies responsible for new teacher placements in Alabama, Rosa again pressed on. Rosa created a public role for herself. She moved to set up a new academic enterprise. The graduate of Payne University did not have to look hard for work:

> At that time, there were in this part of the country some very peculiar local laws pertaining to the public schools in certain districts. One was that if the colored people failed to have a public school for any one scholastic year, the public school money would be returned to the county and be given to the support of the white schools.[9]

In 1909, Rosa developed a plan that allowed her to teach in many schools in Wilcox County. On June 5, 1909, she met with townspeople in Piny Woods, Alabama. She offered to teach a summer school for four months. The people at Piny Woods gladly accepted Rosa's offer to open a school in their community. Many schools in the African American districts ended their sessions at odd times during the year. School terms in Alabama were only three or four months. Rosa lamented that the children had hardly started the term when it was over: "During the long vacation of eight or more months, the children would forget most, if not all, of what they had learned during the previous term."[10]

The school opened in the Coonslide Baptist Church. There were no school buildings for African Americans in central Alabama in the early 1930s. "By any measure . . . the Negro branch of the dual school system lagged far behind. At the end of the Rosenwald building program, which began in 1932, the per-pupil value of Negro school property was less than one-fifth as great as that of white schools."[11] Where there were schools in central Alabama, African American churches operated them. Most of the churches and schools were in poor condition. Rosa recalled students holding umbrellas over her during severe rainstorms while she heard the class recite. The school in Piny Woods remained open until September 1909.

Rosa then moved to Pine Grove, Autauga County, Alabama, in the fall of that year. The Pine Grove school was opened for students on the first Monday in October 1909. At Pine Grove, with the assistance of a "very fine white family," Rosa built her first schoolhouse.[12] At the end of the school term at Pine Grove in 1910, Rosa returned to Piny Woods, where she resumed her school year. The enrollment reached more than one hundred. Rosa had difficulty teaching a diverse group of students with only a few books and no assistance. She was nineteen years old. Unable to secure the support of parents and local townspeople to build a school building, Rosa stopped the Piny Woods project on May 1, 1911. Returning to her hometown of Rosebud, she began the four-month school year. That year, she also taught in Fulton, Alabama.

The African Methodist Episcopal Church offered Rosa two positions in 1911. The Church invited her to work for the Connectional Preachers Aid, an insurance agency, and an AME Book Concern representative. After accepting both positions, she hired a teacher to work in her schools. While serving in these appointments, the AME Church offered Rosa a four-year scholarship to Wilberforce University. Rosa declined the scholarship and returned to teach at Fulton in the fall of 1911.

Establishing an Education Franchise

Rosa devoted her life to helping people in rural Wilcox County, Alabama, lift themselves out of poverty. In 1893, only twenty acres of land in the area were owned by Blacks. The majority of farmers either engaged in sharecropping or leased their land. Sharecropping and leasing made it difficult for farmers to advance their social standing. Leasing and sharecropping placed Black farmers in a cycle of debt. "Enactment of Jim Crow laws in the late 1890s empowered landlords and planters to try to extract more output from tenants and sharecroppers with less compensation rather than using incentives for self-motivated work."[13] Black farmers faced significant challenges due to implementing unjust farm operating contracts imposed by white landlords. Black planters secured loans against their crops to acquire seeds and equipment. Growers frequently found themselves forced to relinquish their small holdings due to a multitude of factors, including crop failures, low selling prices, ill health, poor management, soil exhaustion, excessive interest rates, pressure to sell products at low prices, and the deliberate coordination by white landlords who imposed stringent terms in agricultural contracts.

Rosa's work was similar to her contemporary, William J. Edwards. He was especially concerned about the failure of Blacks to become property owners. Edwards and Rosa worked alongside struggling rural Black farmers to establish education franchises only twelve miles apart. Edwards founded the Snow Hill Normal and Industrial Institute in Wilcox County, Alabama, in a one-room log cabin in 1893, seven years before Rosa launched her project. The Alabama Black Belt counties were home to more than two hundred thousand Blacks, of whom more than 40 percent were of school age, but only one local private school accepted Blacks. Like Rosa, Edwards received no state appropriation for his school. Also, like Rosa, Edwards was gifted land, seven acres, from a local white man who took an interest in his project. Edwards had offers of support from several local churches. He turned them down because he was determined to keep his school free of "isms" and "thoroughly religious in its spirit, but entirely undenominational."[14] Edwards concluded:

> Many times when all was dark, and there seemed to be no way, some of these denominations would come and offer me the

> money to run the work, provided I would accept their faith. But this I have never done; I had rather that the work should die than to sell my principle for money.[15]

Rosa accepted the financial support of Lutherans primarily because she wanted to ensure the survival of her school. The support of Lutherans came with a high cost. William Edwards had more options than Rosa, and turned his attention away from "denominations". Over a short period, Rosa's project underwent a transformation and evolved into a project of the Lutheran Church. The Synodical Conference created a mission board to oversee its "Colored Missions" called "The Mission Board of the Evangelical Lutheran Synodical Conference of North America, for Mission Work Among the Heathen and the Negro."[16] Rosa's Rosebud Literary and Industrial School became part of the first church on the Lutheran Alabama mission field and was rebranded as Christ Lutheran Church and School.

In his memoir, William Edwards notes that the Wilcox County area needed "a school that would endeavor to make education practical rather than theoretical; a school that would train men and women to be good workers, good leaders, good husbands, good wives, and finally train them to be fit citizens of the State and proper subjects for the Kingdom of God."[17] One can see the influence of his mentor, Booker T. Washington.[18] Edwards graduated from Tuskegee in 1893. By 1918, the Snow Hill institute owned 1,940 acres of land and twenty-four buildings and enrolled between three hundred and four hundred students annually. Graduates of the school began to establish similar enterprises throughout the South. Rosa's initiative would progress slowly and only reach its full fruition in the following century.

The Rosebud School

In 1912, Rosa decided to build and conduct a school at Rosebud. With her life savings of two hundred dollars, she intended to create an extraordinary school "which would give little country children a longer school term."[19] Overtures were made to several whites in the Rosebud area for financial assistance. Other fundraising schemes included:

1. Contracting for the public school fund, which was $75.00 for four months. This would help pay the teacher's salary.
2. A local board of trustees was organized with each member contributing $5.00 per year tuition for the children.
3. The parents of each child was charged $1.00 to enter and $0.25 a month tuition.[20]

Rosa next drew plans for a course of study modeled after the one prescribed by the board of education for the Alabama public schools. The only addition to the curriculum was a Bible training course. The core curriculum included reading, writing, spelling, language, history, arithmetic, physiology, and hygiene.

The Rosebud Literary and Industrial School began on July 8, 1912. Recalling the first meeting of the board of directors, Rosa wrote:

> There was no organization; therefore I was obliged to preside. It was not a pleasant thing for a young girl to preside over a body of men, in fact, it was somewhat embarrassing for me.[21]

The panel consisted of eighteen members. Rosa's work was raising money, purchasing land, and raising and capacitating the first school building in Rosebud. While the local school board pledged to do all, they could at the first meeting, Rosa accepted the responsibility of developing a subscription list and going to the homes of selected white people for support.

In her first round of canvassing, she received promises totaling $101.85. To this amount, she added her own two hundred dollars. She then purchased a five-acre plot from her family for fifty dollars. After securing the title to the land, she set out to find lumber for the building. In Pine Apple, she contacted Arthur Lee, owner of a sawmill. "After figuring and figuring, we came to an agreement. He promised to let me have the lumber for $20.00 per thousand. I was to pay down a certain sum and the balance in partial monthly payments."[22] Wagons were then found for transporting the lumber. Brother Nathan R. Ramsey agreed to build the school as a deed of charity for $190.

Rosa opened the Rosebud School on the first Monday of October 1912 near the center of Wilcox Country, twelve miles from Camden, the county seat. The school had forty-five long benches purchased from the African-Methodist Episcopal Church, five heaters, one large school bell, a sewing machine, and 150 Bibles from the American Bible Society. Knox Academy of Selma donated books for the library. Two other women, Lorene Smith and Viola Young, Rosa's sister, combined with Rosa to make a faculty of three. The first year's enrollment reached 155. The school was in session for six months during the first year. At the close of the first year, Rosa went on a "money-begging tour." She needed funding for salaries, books, desks, and repairing leaking roofs and wooden floors. She went with an open hand to the leaders in Alabama's Black communities in Selma, Montgomery, Mobile, and Birmingham. She spoke to lawyers, doctors, professors, bankers, business owners, bishops, and clergy. She solicited many, but few were willing or able to offer help.

In 1913, Rosa began the second term on the first Monday in October. The enrollment reached 215. She hired three additional teachers and expanded the school to fit many students. Eight hundred people attended the closing exercises of the Rosebud school after the seven-month session.

This period of Southern history was challenging for Blacks in Alabama and the nation overall. Rosa opened the school year against continued intimidation and lynching of Blacks. President Woodrow Wilson's first Congress enacted a flood of racist, antiblack legislation. In 1913, Alabama Senator J. Thomas Heflin and Mississippi Senator James Vardaman offered a regular brand of virulent racism in the halls of the US Congress. Among Vardamam's pronouncements: "I am just as opposed to Booker Washington as a voter, with all his Anglo-Saxon reinforcement, as I am to the coconut-headed, chocolate-colored, typical little coon, Andy Dotson, who blacks my shoes every morning. Neither is fit to perform the supreme function of citizenship."[23]

In 1914, cotton farmers all over America witnessed the destruction caused by the Mexican boll weevil invasion. This infestation affected the central Alabama economy, as cotton was the only standard cash crop in the area. Farmers experienced the discontinuation of the extensive credit system by which landlords had advanced tenants' money.[24] The boll weevil wreaked havoc on the region's only cash crop.

When the school at Rosebud opened in 1914, enrollments had fallen drastically, the victims of boll weevil economics. Parents obliged Rosa to accept farm products, since most of them were farmers, as a substitute for the small tuition paid by families; therefore, she had no money to pay teachers. Rosa then had to convert the farm products into money. She writes, "This I had hauled to Camden and sold for what I could get in order to secure money with which to pay our teachers in part."[25] One teacher had to be laid off. The music teacher resigned after the school fell several months behind in paying salaries. Rosa writes, "When the school closed that spring, I had only $12.85 with which to pay salaries. I gave Sister Viola $12.50, and I kept 35 cents for my salary that year. The saddest part of all was that Sister Viola, who had been with me all through school and from the beginning in this school-work, resigned and accepted a position in the city school at Prattville, Ala., at a salary of $60 a month."[26]

Undeterred by the events, Rosa Young determined she would save the school. She met with her board and secured an agreement to cede ownership and operation of the school to the African Methodist Episcopal Church. The African Methodist Episcopal Church refused the offer because of the distance from a major city. The geographical spread of the African Methodist Episcopal before the Civil War was mainly restricted to the northeast and midwest. A significant era of denominational development occurred during the Civil War and Reconstruction with the movement of AME clergy into states, including Alabama, of the collapsing Confederacy, inviting emancipated slaves into their denomination. As early as 1864, the AME Church sent preachers to Mobile, Alabama. While there were rural AME members like Rosa's family, the focus was on larger cities.[27]

Rosa next applied to the Anna Jeans Fund,[28] the Rosenwald Fund,[29] the Slater Fund,[30] the Reformed Presbyterian Church, and the American Presbyterian church. They all refused her requests. Northern philanthropy organizations such as the Rosenwald Fund often required that grants were met with matching funds. "Local African American communities, school districts, and 'white friends' were asked to donate at least the grant amount to the new school. Many African-American communities contributed building materials and labor as their match, holding fish fries, bake sales, and other events to raise funds."[31] They all refused her requests.

Rosa turned in every direction imaginable. From philanthropy, she turned to individuals. Determined not to give up, Rosa wrote another letter. She addressed the letter to Dr. Booker T. Washington at Tuskegee Institute, Tuskegee, Alabama.

> I wrote to Dr. Washington that I felt that he had as much as he could look after in the operation of the Tuskegee Institute, all, therefore, that I asked of him was to give me the names of some individual or association in the North that he thought would help my school live for the benefit of my race. The next day, I mailed my letter, and I prayed and waited for an answer.[32]

Driven by confident hope, she was not stumped when he denied the help she sought. She took a step further. She had a dream, and she held on, hoping that someone or something would help make the dream a reality. On November 13, 1915, she wrote a second letter, dated November 13, 1915, to Emmett J. Scott, Washington's secretary, and executive of Tuskegee.[33] Emmett Jay Scott was a prominent member of the Methodist Episcopal Church. He had direct access not only to Washington but also, through Washington, to the White House. Scott received two presidential appointments between 1901 and 1913: Special Assistant Secretary of War under President Theodore Roosevelt and membership in the United States Liberian Commission under President Howard Taft.[34] Here is the text of that letter:

> Prof. Emmett J. Scott
> Tuskegee Inst. Ala.
>
> Dear friend,
>
> I am writing you in the interest of our rural school here. Owing to flights of the Boll weevil and drought during the summer our farmers in this section failed on their farms. There are numbers of worthy students who are not able to enter school this term. Some of these students are members of the Senior class in this school. In order to help people keep their school running, I am making an appeal to the generous public to help the poor class of students to pay their entrance fee. Some of our white friends paid as high as $10.00 and entered

> 10 colored children. Their entrance fee is $1.00. I hope you will find your way clear and send us as much as $1.00 to enter one colored child in school this term. I am struggling now as [n]ever before to keep this much needed work from closing down. Our regular enrollment is 215, but to this date we are only 67. The regular enrollment of students [who) belongs in this district [is] within 4 miles of the school house. I hope to hear from you.
>
> Yours truly,
> Rosa J. Young[35]

Rosa wrote with passion in her letter to Emmett Scott and fought for her ideas. She wanted schools open for impoverished Black children in her area. Rosa was calling on "friends" to invest in keeping the doors of her "much needed work from closing down." A small contribution of one dollar would benefit as many as 215 students. Rosa, a woman one generation removed from slavery, was an advocate who dared to step into the forefront without the political and social access of Black men to whom she made her appeals. Emmett Scott replied to Rosa on November 27, 1915:

> My dear Madam:
>
> I regret very much that I am unable at this time to make a contribution to your work. This has been a very trying year for all of us here at Tuskegee Institute and I have been compelled to husband very carefully what little income I have received in order to insure protection for those dependent upon me.
>
> I am certainly in sympathy with the work you are carrying on and regret that I cannot be of more service at this time.
>
> Yours very truly
> Emmett J. Scott
> Secretary[36]

In his reply, Booker T. Washington encouraged Rosa to write to Christopher F. Drewes of the Board of Colored Missions of the

Evangelical Lutheran Synodical Conference of North America (a grouping of Lutheran synods). Rosa wrote the following letter to the Lutherans:

> Neenah, Ala. October 27, 1915
> Rev. C. F. Drewes
> St. Louis, Mo.
>
> Dear Friend:
>
> I am writing you concerning a school I have organized. I began teaching here in 1912 with seven pupils in an old hall, where the cattle went for shelter. Since then I have bought five acres of land and erected a four-room school-house thereon beside our chapel, which we are working on now; bought 45 seats, 5 heaters, 1 school bell, 1 sewing-machine, 1 piano, A nice collection of useful books, and 150 New testaments for our Bible-training department.
>
> I am writing to see if your conference will take our school under its auspices. If you will take our school under your auspices, we will give you the land, the school-building, and all its contents so start with. If you cannot take our school, I beg the privilege to appeal to you to give us a donation to help us finish our new chapel. No matter how little, any amount will be cheerfully and thankfully received.
>
> This school is located near the center of Wilcox County, twelve miles from the county-seat, fifty-four miles from Selma, Ala., two miles from the L. and N. Railroad, amid 1,500 Colored people. The region is very friendly, but white and colored are interested in this school. I hope you will see your way clear to aid us.[37]

Drewes dispatched the Reverend Nils J. Bakke, a Norwegian Lutheran pastor and Field Secretary of the Synodical Conference, to investigate. Bakke arrived in Rosebud Saturday evening, December 17, 1915. The next day, the local board voted to turn the school over to the Lutheran Synodical Conference. Rosa had saved her school and secured a place in history as the mother of Black Lutheranism in central Alabama. A few months later, on Palm Sunday, 1916, Young was the first confirmed

Lutheran on the Alabama field and a teacher and mission worker for Christ Lutheran Church and School in Rosebud. Rosa brought the Lutheran church to rural Alabama with the power of a letter. From 1916 onward, Lutheran congregations and schools were established for underserved Black children and families.

Teaching in the Lutheran Educational System

The Lutheran Synodical Conference intended to develop a mission field. On entering Alabama, Lutherans believed they had "one opportunity after another to carry the light of the Gospel of Christ into the darkness of ignorance, superstition, and sin."[38] Rev. Christopher F. Drewes wrote in *Half a Century of Lutheranism among Our Colored People,* "The chief aim of our mission-schools is to impart to the pupils a treasure of religious truths, to make them wise to salvation, and to qualify them to be good citizens, good men and women.[39] Without Lutheran day schools, he believed that "Many of those boys and girls would otherwise have grown up as heathen."[40] Of course, even without Lutheran schools, most Black boys and girls grew up as good citizens.

Lutheran objectives for the school took root immediately. Bakke moved with speed. By Sunday, December 19, the preacher delivered his first sermon. He later described the people who handed the Lutherans a mission field in this manner: "The ignorance here in all matters is simply beyond measure."[41] Bakke believed that whites were superior teachers of their less privileged Southern brothers and sisters, who no doubt had their ideas about Christian worship, labor, and how to live and have their being in communities. On Easter Sunday in 1916, a new Lutheran mission baptized fifty-eight persons and confirmed seventy. On Easter Day, a congregation was organized with 117 baptized members, seventy confirmed, and twenty-two voting members.[42]

Nils Bakke then changed the school from a private school to a Christian day school. He organized the first Sunday school and formed classes for baptism and confirmation. Using the Christian day school as a pattern for mission outreach, the growth of Lutheranism in Central Alabama was rapid. At the end of 1926, or ten years after entry into Alabama, the Synodical Conference had twenty-seven day schools with 1,466 pupils enrolled.[43] The schools were frequently led by white pastors who were insufficiently qualified for roles in elementary education. The pastors brought limited and often no understanding of cross-cultural relationships. The schools offered no more than the bare essentials of grade school education, heavily emphasizing religion and Lutheran doctrine.

Quoting census data from 1920, Christopher Drewes makes an astonishing observation: "The death rate among the colored people of this country was 18 per thousand in that year." Then he asserts that in the African American Lutheran churches, the death rate of people of color was only 9 per thousand. "This surprisingly low death rate is an evidence of the complete change of heart and the experience by the colored people when they become real Lutherans. Such persons are completely changed, leading an altogether different life. God fulfills His promises for them, the promise 'that it mayest be well with thee and thou mayest live long on the earth.' Yes, it pays to be real Lutheran."[44] Drewes's simplistic and flawed use of data and conviction of the consequences of Lutheranism was rooted in racism and the belief that improving the moral condition of Blacks would change their lives. Gomes Eanes de Zurara wrote that captured Africans had "lived like beasts, without any custom of reasonable beings . . . [and] only knew how to live in bestial sloth."[45] Once enslaved, their souls may be saved and their lives enriched, he said. Drewes seems to be traveling in the footsteps of De Zurara. However, Lutheran missional activities failed to address or account for justice issues such as inadequate housing, impoverishment, absence of healthcare, and racial subjugation. Although Blacks of Alabama suffered, Drewes believes their lives were saved through conversion to Lutheranism. Drews provided so-called evidence which lay claim to the success of being a "real Lutheran."

The best Lutheran schools never reached minimum standards on their finest days and were subject to financial malnutrition. Most were primitive one-room frame structures, completely lacking in modern facilities. The structures were built with rough pine boards. The pews were homemade slat benches. The chancel furniture and school desk were also homemade from mill-run pine boards abundant in Alabama. Thus, the cost could be kept within the limitation of the board's budget.[46]

The objectives of the Lutheran Synodical Conference of North America in establishing mission schools were very different from

Rosa's objectives. Rosa offered distinct reasons for making education her life's work and establishing the Rosebud Literary and Industrial School. Anchored in the educational theories of Johann Heinrich Pestalozzi, a Swiss pedagogue and educational reformer who exemplified Romanticism in his approach, following the work of Jean-Jacques Rousseau, was the belief in a whole-child approach that focused on the head, heart, and hands.[47] Education was a vehicle for creating a more just society. Rosa writes,

> One day at recess . . . the thought came to my mind to build a large school in the country which would give the little children a longer school term to run the school on a cheap basis that would enable the poorest boys and girls endowed with bright intellects, but not able to defray their expenses in other schools to obtain a higher education; to establish a school that would give the youth of my race a real, true, three-fold education of the head, the hand, and the heart.[48]

Rosa's pioneering work as an educator resulted far beyond her original intent. The swift growth of the Alabama mission school necessitated the formation of a high school and college. In 1919, the Alabama Luther Conference petitioned the Synodical Conference to develop such a school. According to one report, this was a remarkable and timely decision: "As late as 1920, 85 percent of all Negro pupils in the South were enrolled in the first four grades."[49] In 1916, there were "only 67 Negro public high schools, with fewer than 20,000 students."[50] The Synodical Conference granted the petition to open the new school in 1920, and in 1922, the city of Selma, on the Alabama River, was chosen as the future home of the new high school and college.

In the spring of 1925, the Mission Board bought thirteen acres of land in the northeastern part of Selma for $12,300. There was a small cottage on the ground. The dormitory and recitation hall, erected during the summer of 1925, cost about $36,000. The school employed Rosa J. Young as matron of the girl's dormitory. The school was dedicated on Sunday afternoon, September 20, 1925.[51] Alabama Lutheran Academy and College started in a dwelling at 520 First Avenue. The school was renamed Concordia College Alabama in 1981 and was part of the Concordia University System of the Lutheran Church—Missouri

Synod. Concordia College Alabama, Selma, held the distinction as the nation's only Historically Black Lutheran College. For 99 years, the school provided affordable education to young men and women from its founding in 1922 until its closure in 2018.

Legacy

Awarded an Honorary Doctorate of Literary Letters by Concordia Theological Seminary, Springfield, Illinois, in May 1961, Rosa was both the first woman and the first African American to be honored in this way by the Lutheran Church—Missouri Synod. Rosa Young offered a project that benefited not only herself but her community and beyond. Facing Jim Crow segregation, deep poverty, isolation, discrimination, and hardship, Young initiated an educational effort that led to the founding of thirty parochial schools for African American students in communities across Alabama from 1912 to 1960. She was a woman who left a footprint on education in Alabama communities during her lifetime. The widespread migration of African Americans in the twentieth century from rural communities in the South to large cities in the North and West led to the decline of rural communities.[52] "The exodus of African-American Lutherans from Alabama seeded Lutheran congregations across the country. In 1977, 35 African-American pastors in the LCMS could trace their roots to the Alabama Field."[53] Rosa schools educated thousands of children who needed schools and prepared leaders in ministry, education, civil rights, and law. In 2016, the Lutheran Church—Missouri Synod made a documentary on her life titled *The First Rosa*.[54] The film details her long odds and struggles with strident critics, the Ku Klux Klan, and even the invasion of boll weevils. Buried at Christ Lutheran Church, Rosebud, Alabama, Rosa Young died on June 30, 1971.

Notes

1. Rosa J. Young, *Light in the Dark Belt* (St. Louis: Concordia Publishing House, 1929), 15.
2. Calvin Patterson, *Patterson's Common School Speller* (New York: Sheldon & Company, 1882).

3. Young, *Light in the Dark Belt*, 16.
4. Payne University operated from 1889 to 1979. The college was originally founded in Selma in 1889. Its campus was located at 1525 Franklin Street. The college operated at that location through 1922, when it relocated to the city of Birmingham. The college was located at 6415 Washington Boulevard. By 1974, the college had to be relocated because of airport expansion and the building of interstate highways in the area. The street on which the college was located no longer exists; however, a remnant of University Avenue that once led to the campus connects to the Messer Airport Highway. The college moved to a new campus at the southeast corner of Cherry Avenue and Daniel Payne Drive on the far northern edge of Birmingham, where new buildings were constructed in 1974. On April 4, 1977 a destructive tornado tore through the campus, severely damaging buildings. The damage, along with mounting financial problems, forced the school to file for bankruptcy in 1978 and close its doors in 1979. At the time of its closure, the college had 120 students enrolled on the 153 acres campus.
5. Young, *Light in the Dark Belt*, 28.
6. Young, *Light in the Dark Belt*, 31.
7. Young, *Light in the Dark Belt*, 32.
8. Young, *Light in the Dark Belt*, 34.
9. Young, *Light in the Dark Belt*, 40.
10. Young, *Light in the Dark Belt*, 50.
11. Harry S. Ashmore, *The Negro and the Schools* (Chapel Hill: University of North Carolina Press, 1954), 17.
12. Young, *Light in the Dark Belt*, 42.
13. Ian D. Ochiltree, "'A Just and Self-Respecting System'? Black Independence, Sharecropping, and Paternalistic Relations in the American South and South Africa." *Agricultural History*, 72, no. 2 (Spring 1998): 352–380.
14. William J. Edwards, *Twenty-Five Years in The Dark Belt* (Boston: The Cornhill Company, 1918), 43.
15. Edwards, *Twenty-Five Years in The Dark Belt*, 43.
16. Christopher Drewes, *Half a Century of Lutheranism among Our Colored People* (St. Louis: Concordia Publishing House, 1927), 11.
17. Drewes, *Half a Century of Lutheranism among Our Colored People*, 35
18. Margaret O'Brien, "William J Edwards, Black Educator—Cyclopedia" at https://exploreblackheritage.com/william-j-edwards-black-educator/. Retrieved February 5, 2023.
19. Drewes, *Half a Century of Lutheranism among Our Colored People*, 47.
20. Drewes, *Half a Century of Lutheranism among Our Colored People*, 64–65.

21. Drewes, *Half a Century of Lutheranism among Our Colored People*, 65.
22. Drewes, *Half a Century of Lutheranism among Our Colored People*, 72–73.
23. *Ebony Pictorial History of Black America* (Chicago: Johnson Publishing Company, 1971), 103.
24. Young, *Light in the Dark Belt*, 82.
25. Young, *Light in the Dark Belt*, 84.
26. Young, *Light in the Dark Belt*, 84.
27. Dennis C. Dickerson, "Our History," https://www.ame-church.com/our-church/our-history/. Retrieved, February 9, 2023.
28. Cheryl Knott Malone. "Jeans, Anna Thomas (07 April 1822—24 September 1907)," *American National Biography*. https://doi.org/10.1093/anb/9780198606697.article.0900387. Retrieved March 30, 2019.
29. Ashmore, *The Negro and the Schools*, 17.
30. August Meier, *Negro Thought in America 1880–1915: Racial Ideologies in the Age of Booker T. Washington* (University of Michigan Press, 1963), 90.
31. Rebekah Dobrasko. *Northern Money, Southern Schools: The Rosenwald School Fund*. https://scdah.sc.gov/sites/scdah/files/Documents/Historic%20Preservation%20(SHPO)/For%20teachers/NorthernMoneyCurriculum.pdf
32. Young, *Light in the Dark Belt*, 90.
33. W. A. Low and V. A. Clift. *Encyclopedia of Black America* (New York: Da Capo Press, 1981), 748.
34. Dictionary of American Biography. (PDF). www.morgan.edu. Archived from the original (PDF) on January 1, 2011. Retrieved April 4, 2019.
35. Reel 288 of the Micro-film edition of the Library of Congress. Manuscript Division, "Booker T. Washington Papers."
36. Ibid.
37. Drewes, *Half a Century of Lutheranism among Our Colored People*, 56.
38. Drewes, *Half a Century of Lutheranism among Our Colored People*, 59.
39. Drewes, *Half a Century of Lutheranism among Our Colored People*, 70.
40. Drewes, *Half a Century of Lutheranism among Our Colored People*, 71.
41. Drewes, *Half a Century of Lutheranism among Our Colored People*, 57.
42. Drewes, *Half a Century of Lutheranism among Our Colored People*, 58.
43. Drewes, *Half a Century of Lutheranism among Our Colored People*, 66.
44. Drewes, *Half a Century of Lutheranism among Our Colored People*, 71–72.
45. Marcelo E. Fuentes. "'Crespo e Nuu e Negro': Gomes Eanes de Zurara and the Racialization of Non-Christians by Portuguese Authors." *Essays in Medieval Studies*, 34 (2018), 17–38. https://doi.org/10.1353/ems.2018.0001.

46. Walter H. Ellwanger, "Lutheranism in Alabama and Other Parts of the South," *Concordia Historical Institute Quarterly*, 48, no. 2 (Summer 1975), 38.
47. A. Brühlmeier, *Head, Heart and Hand: Education in the Spirit of Pestalozzi* (Cambridge: Sophia Books, 2010).
48. Young, *Light in the Dark Belt*, 59.
49. Ashmore, *The Negro and the Schools*, 19.
50. Ashmore, *The Negro and the Schools*, 19.
51. Drewes, *Half a Century of Lutheranism among Our Colored People*, 93.
52. https://www.britannica.com/event/Great-Migration. Retrieved March 10, 2023.
53. Richard Dickinson, *Roses and Thorns: The Centennial Edition of Black Lutheran Mission and Ministry in The Lutheran Church–Missouri Synod* (St. Louis: Concordia Publishing House, 1977) 69–71.
54. The First Rosa, https://www.youtube.com/watch?v=9PFC68Zcpgs

CHAPTER 5

Sister Emma Francis

The First Black Lutheran Deaconess to Serve in the West Indies

ROSA J. YOUNG was not the only Black woman in this hemisphere to leave a significant imprint on American Lutheranism. In Holy Trinity Lutheran Church Cemetery in Frederiksted, US Virgin Islands, is the grave of Emma H. F. Francis. The inscription reads:

IN SACRED MEMORY OF SISTER EMMA H. F. FRANCIS
LUTHERAN DEACONESS
BORN Dec. 7, 1875, ST. KITTS. B.W.I.
DIED APRIL 8, 1945 ST. CROIX, V.I.
Her life of Christian service has benefited many. God be praised.[1]

Early Life and Education

Emma Hermina Francisca Francis was a native of St. Kitts in the British West Indies. She was the daughter of Rev. Joseph Franklin Francis, a Moravian minister, and Mary Henrietta Francis. The Moravian missionaries and the Royal Danish Mission College were the first large-scale Protestant missionary movement. A long line of Moravian missionaries crossed the Atlantic Ocean from Germany to convert enslaved Africans on the islands. The Moravians were the first Protestant denomination to minister to slaves. When Emma was 15, she entered teacher training at a Moravian school in Antigua.[2]

After her studies in Antigua, Emma returned to St. Kitts to work alongside her father at the Estridge Mission, where Reverend Francis was pastor. A parochial school connected to the mission provided Emma with a classroom. Emma and her older sister assisted with the work of the mission. Her mother was getting older and ill, so Emma and her sister did most of the housework. Emma gave up teaching as her mother needed more assistance and began navigating the tricky road of primary caregiving. While Emma cared for her mother, her older sister taught and visited the flock in their father's church. Reverend Francis also became ill, and "the two sisters passed many anxious nights by their bedside."[3]

Missionary Work

After her mother's death, Emma followed through on a process of discernment. Her call to become a missionary became unmistakably clear. Her eldest brother, a Moravian pastor and a student in Germany, invited her to consider studying there. She wrote to the director of the Bible House at Bad Freinwalde, a town in the Märkisch-Oderland district in Brandenburg, Germany, asking to be admitted to this school, which trained women for missionary work. She was accepted. She arrived on Good Friday and was sent to Berlin by the Moravian brethren.[4] In Berlin, Emma was greeted by her brother. She spent a few months with missionaries in West Prussia, learning the German language, and accompanied her brother to lectures.

Immediately upon arrival in Freinwalde she entered the Bible House, a learning and worship community. Her brother soon left for Demerara in British Guiana. At Freinwalde, Emma's studies included courses in nursing at the Elizabeth Hospital in Berlin. The hospital was named after Queen Elisabeth of Prussia and was established in 1843. It began as a children's hospital in Mitte but then moved to Oberschöneweide (Karlshorster Straße at the time, now Treskowallee) and expanded to include a department for internal medicine and surgery for adults.

At the end of her studies, the mission board considered Emma for mission work in Sudan. The school's mission board denied posting her there because they feared she would not be accepted since she was "colored" and wouldn't be considered an equal to white missionaries. Distinct understandings of racial capabilities, and racialism shaped the views of the mission board. The board saw Emma as different. They could not see how people of different backgrounds and skin colors could learn from each other, share skills, and serve together. The mission board suggested she follow her brother to Demerara.

Emma's Plan A was to be a missionary. But she also had a Plan B: the deaconess movement in Germany. Emma gave up plans for mission work. The mission board would not support her candidacy for missionary work because she would not be considered equal to white missionaries. What the board saw as a lack of ability in Emma translated into a lack of opportunity for her. Emma's success as a missionary depended on the support of a white Lutheran denomination and the cooperation of white missionary colleagues. Those colleagues shaped a missionary enterprise that kept Blacks separated from whites. Emma's story adds depth and complication to the sometimes too-simple narrative of mission history. She resolved to find other ways of serving and looked for new opportunities.

Deaconess Work

In 1906, she was invited to the Deaconess House in Friendenshort by Sister Eva von Winkle. The Deaconess House Friedenshort was active in social-diaconal projects all over Germany in youth welfare services, working with the disabled and the elderly, and in some social and missionary projects abroad. Sister Eva and Emma formed a long-time friendship.

Fridenshort was a large institution that trained deaconesses and gave them service opportunities. The modern deaconess movement began in Germany in 1836 when Lutheran Pastor Theodor Fliedner and his wife Friederike Münster opened the first deaconess motherhouse in Kaiserswerth on the Rhine.[5] The deaconesses opened homes for orphans, widows, and the poor and infirm, preached the gospel in women's prisons, and set up homes where these women could live when discharged. Emma was impressed with the work that deaconesses were doing in Germany. Here was an opportunity for Christian service that could utilize all her talents. Emma, modeling her work after Phoebe, named in Romans 16:1–2, was prepared to serve in various roles: as a teacher, visitor to the sick, spiritual caregiver, serving in hospitals, prisons, orphanages, complementing the word and sacrament ministry of an ordained pastor. At the end of her training, Emma became a deaconess. She received the garb of a deaconess in 1907, the typical attire of the church's servants, and the title of Sister. She was commissioned for service at one of the three orphanages of Queen Louise Home for Children on St. Croix, Danish Virgin Islands.

From Germany to Danish Colony in the Caribbean

Beginning in 1666, the Danish began to execute plans for a Danish colony in the Caribbean. The Danish West Indies' economy depended on slavery because sugar was the main crop for trade. Danish Lutheran missional work was closely aligned with the Danish colony. Danish settlers established congregations under a charter by the royal government. This charter included a provision that the Lutheran Church (the state religion of Denmark) was to be maintained in the colony, and the company was to select appropriate ministers to serve it.

> When St. Thomas became a crown colony through purchase of the company by the State in 1754, the church was able to expand its role in community affairs very rapidly. Already it was operating schools for Lutheran children and later for slave children as well. It was a Lutheran Pastor, the Rev. Hans Stoud, who first proposed that a hospital and school should be built on each island and saw his proposal realized on St. Thomas. Thanks to the laborious efforts of Pastor Erik Wold and Mr. J. M. Magens (a Dane born on St. Thomas and of the same family after whom Magens Bay is named), Luther's Small Catechism, a hymnal and grammar were all printed in the Creole language by 1770.[6]

By the 1750s the Lutherans were doing mission work with the enslaved Africans on the islands. After a slave rebellion, slavery was officially abolished in 1848, leading to the near economic collapse of the plantations, along with the sugar industry being plagued by drought and political and economic uncertainty in Europe.

After emancipation in 1848, freed blacks were paid subsistence wages. In 1902, the Danish Government established a commission "to study the economic, social and racial condition in the islands with a view towards reform."[7] Among the agenda items taken up by the commission were issues of infant mortality and the care of sick children. At the heart of the government's concern was the need to grow strong and healthy Black children ready to go into the labor force, into "the field or elsewhere on the estates" to work so that colonists would not have to import workers.[8] In 1904, Crown Princess Louise of Denmark, working with the West Indian Committee for Child Care, organized a plan to open a childcare center in Frederiksted in cooperation with Pastor N. P. Nygaard of the Lutheran Church in Frederiksted who developed the original plan for a childcare program. The childcare center opened in Frederiksted under the direction of two Danish deaconesses with support from the Women Mission Workers of the Danish Lutheran Church.

Beginning in December 1906, Olga Fanny baroness Schaffalitzky de Muckadell, a leader of the Women Mission Workers of the Danish Lutheran Church, spent six months in the Danish West Indies. Observing the poverty on the islands, she raised funds for a childcare center. She also obtained the assistance of Sister Eva von Winkle of the Deaconess House Friendenshort in finding a qualified worker to run the Ebenezer Orphanage for Girls in Frederiksted. Eva recommended Sister Emma Francis. Emma spent several months in Denmark, was commissioned by the Danish Lutheran Church (Church of Denmark) for service in St. Croix. She was appointed for service at one of the three orphanages run by Queen Louise Home on St. Croix. Shortly after commissioning, Emma sailed home. She became the first Black deaconess to serve in North America and the first Lutheran deaconess from the West Indies. Emma was able to use her training as a teacher and nurse and her administration skills. She served at the orphanage for nearly forty years, touching the lives of hundreds of children in the Virgin Islands.

In 1917, Denmark sold its colony to the United States for $25 million and retreated from the Caribbean after a legacy of nearly two and a half centuries. The United States, the new managers of the islands, was permeated with specific notions about race and was perceived as unsympathetic and tough in their approach toward the local population. Today, "Together with Guam and Puerto Rico, these islands linger in a colonial system."[9] The United States Virgin Islands has been on the United Nations list of Non-Self-Governing Territories since 1946. The Lutheran Homes on the islands were transferred to the General Council of the Evangelical Lutheran Church in North America (the General Council). The General Council was the predecessor to the United Lutheran Church in America, formed in 1918. According to *Lutheran Women's Work* magazine, the Lutheran Homes were "deeded to the General Council, and accepted for them by their Commissioner appointed at the last convention of the General Council."[10] Most of the Danish deaconesses returned to Denmark. Sister Emma and Sister Maren Knudsen remained, along with Johanna Siverstsen.

By 1920, two Queen Louise homes were at capacity serving about sixty children—including the sick wards and the daycare center, plus the kindergartens. The governing board of the Lutheran Church in America urged that the older girls needed skills training that included necessary competencies for personal advancement—giving them the tools required to succeed in life. The Lutherans in the United States also were concerned about illegitimate births:

> An orphanage for girls is the most blessed of charities in a land where 70 percent of the births are illegitimate. Under the Christian influence of one of their own race, Deaconess Sister Emma Francis, these orphan girls are given a chance in life which would be utterly impossible without this noble institution founded by K.M.A. (Women's Missionary Society of Denmark) . . . There are seventeen girls in the Home, and by the faithful co-operation with Sister Emma, we have been able to conduct the Home on a very economic basis. By their own labors, breaking bread for the hospital, they have been able to provide a fund for needed improvements, and from which also the girls, when leaving the orphanage, are given a proper outfit with which to enter the world.[11]

Of course, legitimacy cannot be taken away from a child. Children are not illegal or unlawful because they are unacknowledged by a parent. The "illegitimate" label used by Lutherans in the United States gave support to the view that some children are "legitimate" and others are not. The term denigrates children. However, through Emma's work children were provided a stable environment at Queen Louise Home. Children received food, shelter, clothing, and education. The years that followed established Queen Louise Home in the community and were marked by rapid growth. Three years after its opening the Danish Lutheran Church purchased additional property both in Christiansted and Frederiksted. No. 57 Queen Street in Christiansted would serve as a second childcare center and the property at No. 24–27 Hospital Street in Frederiksted expanded the original home, becoming the Ebenezer Orphanage for girls. The three homes provided care and nurturing in a homelike atmosphere.

From the West Indies to New York

In 1921, Sister Emma took a leave of absence for rest. Sister Emma initially traveled to Harlem for rest, however, "there was a growing movement urging the West Indies Mission Board to reduce its involvement in the islands and devote more time and resources to a ministry for the 120,000 West Indians who had moved to New York City's Harlem."[12] There was need for a mission to Lutheran Virgin Islanders living in New York. Sister Emma was received by the Deaconess Board as a deaconess of the United Lutheran Church and assigned as parish deaconess in Harlem. Sister Emma was tapped by the Mission Board of the United Lutheran Church in America to lead this new missional undertaking. She agreed. Emma was now in the company of the first wave of Virgin Islanders who migrated to New York. Sister Emma began work in Harlem in 1922. An account of those migrations is preserved in *Lutheran Women's Work*:

> While investigating the field our commissioners were constantly petitioned to do something for the West Indians in New York City. Evidence was produced indicating that many hundreds had gone to New York City within memory of the present generation, of which very few had found homes in established churches. The matter was carefully considered by the Board, which felt that it was obligated by the duties imposed upon it by its constitution, to care for these West Indians in New York City. After notifying the Home Mission Board, the Executive Secretary was authorized to investigate the matter and if possible provide for the spiritual need of

> these West Indians. From the beginning the work has grown by leaps and bounds, and although worshipping in quarters rented from the Y.M.C.A. with the Sunday School held at 7 p.m. and church at 8 p.m., the attendance at church services at the date of this report, August 14, was running over 100 each Sunday.

Sister Emma was soon joined by Sister Edith Prince who was enrolled in the Deaconess Training School at the Mary J. Drexel Motherhouse in Philadelphia. At the time of her enrollment, plans were underway for the establishment of a motherhouse for the training of colored deaconesses in Harlem.[13] In a report written by Sister Emma about New York City, she wrote:

> Oh, there are so many sad, wounded, and despairing hearts everywhere to be cheered and comforted . . . Sometimes it is a mother whose husband has deserted her and his children or has proved indifferent and neglectful; children whose disobedience and waywardness cause their parents much worry and anxiety; and, it was in one case, a young mother who asked me for advice and guidance in managing home affairs and conquering the difficulties there.[14]

In 1926 Sister Emma was hit by a taxicab and seriously injured. After a lengthy period of hospitalization and recuperation, she returned to the Virgin Islands in 1927 to resume her role as administrator of Ebenezer Home.

Legacy

In honor of Sister Emma Francis's achievements, Sister Emma Cottage was constructed at Queen Louise Home in 1996 by the Lutheran Services of the Virgin Islands. At that time Queen Louise Home began to receive many requests for placement of children with severe physical and developmental disabilities. The children required an intensive level of care not possible in the home's standard cottages, so this special cottage opened to accommodate children with severe disabilities and was named after Sister Emma.

Notes

1. http://dkconsulateusvi.com/HDC/stCroix/frederiksted/frederiksted.html. Retrieved March 21, 2017.
2. Catherine B. Herzel, *She Made Many Rich: Sister Emma Francis* (Friendship Press, 1948), 5.
3. Herzel, *She Made Many Rich*, 6.
4. Herzel, *She Made Many Rich*, 7.
5. Theodor Fliedner (1800–1864) was a German Lutheran minister and founder of Lutheran deaconess training. In 1836, he founded Kaiserswerther Diakonie, a hospital and deaconess training center. He is commemorated as a renewer of society in the Calendar of Saints of the Evangelical Lutheran Church in America on October 4 and by the Evangelical Church in Germany on October 5.
6. The Lutheran Church. http://www.dkconsulateusvi.com/hdc/stThomas/thelutheranchurch/thelutheranchurch.html. Retrieved June 17, 2017.
7. Juanita Lawson-Haith and Susan Ellis, *It All Began with Children: The First Century of Queen Louise Home and Lutheran Social Services in the Virgin Islands, 1904 to 2004*. (Lutheran Social Services of The Virgin Islands, Frederiksted), 5.
8. Minutes of Colonial Council Meeting, August 18, 1903. Danish National Archives, Copenhagen. West India and Guinea Company's Archives, 1755–1917.
9. Alex Bryne. *Yes, the US had an Empire—And in The Virgin Islands, It Still Does*. The Conversation, Africa Edition. (2017). Retrieved from https://theconversation.com/yes-the-us-had-an-empire-and-in-the-virgin-islands-it-still-does-73567
10. *Lutheran Women's Work*, 15 (May 1922): 227
11. *Lutheran Women's Work*, 15 (May 1922): 227.
12. *Lutheran Women's Work*, 15 (May 1922): 23.
13. *Lutheran Women's Work*, 15 (May 1922): 193.
14. Herzel, *She Made Many Rich*, 17.

CHAPTER 6

Nelson Trout

The First African American Lutheran Bishop

> If you know whence you came, there is really no limit to where you can go.
>
> —James Baldwin

THROUGHOUT HIS MINISTRY, Nelson W. Trout never lost touch with his upbringing in Black churches. His sermon delivery pattern was in keeping with the preaching styles of his father and mother, a technique practiced primarily among African Americans in the Black Church. Trout's "call and respond" preaching provided room for the congregation to answer. Trout preached messages that appealed to his hearers' intellect and expressive dimensions. The preaching is rooted in the harrowing experiences of Blacks during slavery in the United States and experiences during the Jim Crow period and ensuing discrimination.

Early Life

Nelson Wesley Trout was born to William and Bertha Alston Trout on September 29, 1920, in Columbus, Ohio. William and Bertha had five sons and three daughters.[1] Nelson grew up in Urbancrest, right outside Columbus. A reliable Trout family history is impossible mainly due to limited records, but this was typical for other families then. William Trout Sr. served as chairman of the Deacon Board of Union Baptist Church, founded in 1822. He was also Urbancrest's first City Council president.

Nelson describes his father as a "hard shell" Baptist. Bertha Alston Trout, his mother, was a Pentecostal preacher. He writes, "Growing up in that household, often my job was to referee. Reflecting her Christian experience, my mother always prayed for me to speak in tongues, all my brothers and sisters did." Trout followed his father into the Baptist Church. He was ordained a Baptist minister in 1947.

Education and Theological Training

Trout spent his first year of college at Wilberforce University, Zenia, Ohio, an African American College whose first president was Daniel Payne (see chapter 2). Like Daniel Payne, who joined the Lutheran Church while a seminary student, Nelson Trout began his journey into Lutheranism while in the academy. Both Payne and Trout eventually became bishops. At the end of his studies at Wilberforce, Trout enrolled at Capital University, Columbus, Ohio. At Capital, he met Rev. Erwin Krebs, who invited Trout to become a Lutheran.[2]

Image 6.1. Trout Family Members, date unknown. Nelson W. Trout is standing on the left. His father and mother are seated in the center.

With an invitation to membership from Lutherans, Trout graduated with a Bachelor of Arts from Capital University in 1948. Following graduation, he applied for admission to Evangelical Lutheran Theological Seminary (Renamed Trinity Lutheran Seminary in 1978) in Columbus, Ohio. Trout wrote, "They were willing to take a risk and take in some non-Lutherans like me." The Columbus years at Evangelical Lutheran Theological Seminary were good years for Nelson. Trout connected and built rapport with professors.

> When I came to the seminary, I didn't intend to become a Lutheran. I came here to convert all the other people. But I took classes and debated (often quite vigorously) with theologians such as Dr. Theodore Liefield and Dr. Jacob Dell. They made such an impression on me that I knew I wanted to be a Lutheran.

Through studies, discernment, and engagement with professors and learning peers, Trout discovered compelling reasons for becoming a Lutheran. During an interview at an event honoring him at Trinity Lutheran Seminary in January 1991, an audience member asked Trout, "Is it possible to be African American and Lutheran?"[3] Responding in the affirmative, Trout asked, "Do we have to give up something?" Trout was referring to issues of identity and culture. "Do we turn our backs on those things and reach out to a new culture to be adopted?" Trout pondered what it means to be loyal to one's own culture while at the same time celebrating the religious experience of another culture. Trout concluded that Blacks can be present in and among people of different cultures and "be loyal to our own culture." For Trout, the question was, How can two seemingly divergent realities be harmonized so that the effect of the relationship blesses everybody? His response: "Christianity is colorblind and does not pander to racial distinctions." Yet, Trout was not unaware of the fact that colorblindness may be taken to the extreme. Colorblindness may erase people's color altogether, where someone is no longer black, but just our "friend." Trout engaged in the discussion of Black presence in Lutheranism throughout his ministry.

Nelson Trout graduated from Evangelical Lutheran Theological Seminary in 1952. He completed additional academic study at Ohio State University, Columbus, Ohio, and the School of Religion,

University of Southern California, Los Angeles, California. In 1982, he spent a three-month sabbatical studying Latin American theology at the Higher Institute of Theological Study in Buenos Aires, Argentina. Trout studied with José Míguez Bonino, a Latin American liberation theology founder. He read, discussed, and valued the writings of the Argentinian scholar. The experience in Argentina was a seminal moment for Trout. He self-identified for the rest of his life as a liberation theologian. Trout was attracted to liberation theology's emphasis on the liberation of the oppressed and its social concern for the poor. He found in liberation theology a systematic expression of the faith that his experiences had not provided. Trout believed that liberation theology attempted to make the gospel politically respectable. These became themes in Trout's preaching and lectures.

Trout used his understanding of Latin American liberation theology as a bridge to Black theology, a movement initiated by James Cone in the second half of the 1960s. Black theology and liberation theology complemented Trout's efforts in fighting injustice against Blacks. He gained notoriety at the Lutheran World Federation meeting in 1954 in Budapest, Hungary.[4] With an eloquent denunciation of two white southern African churches, the Evangelical Lutheran Church Southern Africa (Cape Church) and the German Evangelical Lutheran Church in South West Africa, Trout critiqued the churches for their failure to oppose apartheid. After debate, the white churches were later suspended from membership in the Lutheran World Federation.[5]

While liberation theologies originate in fighting oppression, inequality, and dehumanizing contexts, such as poverty, racism, misogyny, ableism, and homophobia, Trout struggled to articulate a straightforward approach to the LGBTQIA+ community under his care as Bishop of the South Pacific District. "Don't expect me to give a rationale for the way they are," Trout said, referring to gay and lesbian people. But he urged congregations to be "in conversation with these people and open your doors."[6] In a district that included San Francisco and conservative communities in Orange County, there were convention resolutions targeting the participation of gay and lesbian people. "Exclusion from church fellowship is not an option for us," Trout told delegates. While the District adopted anti-LGBTQIA+ resolutions, opposed by Trout, he supported churches holding membership in "Reconciling in Christ" (Reconciling Works), an independent,

Lutheran membership-supported organization.[7] Like many in the Lutheran Church, Trout's understanding and thinking on LGBTQIA+ matters was emerging.

Pastoral Work

Trout enlisted in the United States Army and served active duty in the infantry during the Second World War from 1939 to 1946. He was commissioned as a second lieutenant at the Army Infantry School in 1942 and promoted to first lieutenant in the Army Chaplains Corps in 1958. Trout completed his military service as a Captain in 1960 and entered the inactive reserves until 1967.

After separating from the military and completing a Master of Theology degree at age 31, Nelson was ready for his first assignment as a Lutheran pastor. This period began Nelson Trout's long career in the Lutheran Church in the United States. He was invited in 1952 to serve as pastor of Trinity Lutheran Church in Montgomery, Alabama. Trinity was a small congregation with a parochial school. It was "supported as a mission by the National Lutheran Council and was "the only decent school available to Negroes," and according to Trout, "many ambitious families had swallowed their distaste for the staid Lutheran liturgy in order to educate their children."[8] Lutheran worship was different from worship in traditional Black churches. The call-and-response preaching style was missing in Lutheran churches in the United States. Lutherans prayed prayers using worship books, not spontaneously or "from the heart." Blacks in Montgomery may have found Lutheran worship formal and abstract rather than experiential and dynamic. While African Americans, in worship, may comprehend a lot, they also want to feel something, namely God's Spirit.[9] They desire to know God personally rather than learn about God through doctrines, creeds, traditions, and art, and they frown on the mere recitation of dogmas as proof that God is known. What matters most is to know God through God's revelational activities in their personal and corporate lives.[10] The Black worship tradition shaped Trout's early faith formation.

Trout arrived in Montgomery at a time of civil unrest. The year he arrived was the year Jeremiah Reeves, a Black 16-year-old, was accused of raping a white woman in the city.[11] The fight to free Reeves was the primary focus of NAACP efforts when Martin Luther King Jr., then 25, arrived in Montgomery in 1954. Another situation creating tension was that whites in Montgomery in the 1950s reacted to the court-ordered integration of public schools and maintained a segregated school systems by establishing private educational franchises. At one point, Montgomery had more private schools than any other city in America. White children could avoid attending schools with African Americans. Nelson Trout's arrival in Alabama coincided with the moment when the flames of the civil rights movement in Montgomery began to ignite. He was active in the movement through activism and his ministry.

A Lutheran Presence in Montgomery

Primarily through the Lutheran Synodical Conference of North America, Lutherans were involved in ministry to the African American community beginning in 1877.[12] The Conference founded missions, parochial schools, and three schools of college grade. Lutherans conducted missional work in Alabama, Arkansas, Louisiana, North Carolina, and Texas. When Trout arrived in Montgomery, Alabama, the Lutheran Bible Institute, organized by the American Lutheran Church, held classes in a rented house near Alabama State College, a historically Black college. Alabama Lutheran Bible Institute was launched by the American Lutheran Church in 1947 when the Martin Luther Institute of Tuscaloosa, Alabama, was merged with the Alabama Lutheran Bible Institute of Montgomery. The reasons for the establishment of this school are sketchy. According to a report from the Board of Colored Missions of the American Lutheran Church, a plan to send Black students to Northern colleges and seminaries was unsuccessful. Students who had gone to Woodville, Ohio (Woodville Normal School), Columbus, Ohio (Capitol University and Evangelical Lutheran Seminary), and Waverly, Iowa (Wartburg College) for teacher and ministerial education had failed. There are only anecdotal reasons stated to explain why the students failed to achieve academically. One reason cited was the students "had been taken out of their proper environment."[13] This reason, of course, was nonsense when it was written.

During this period of United States history, the Great Migration was occurring. More than six million African Americans moved from the rural southern United States to the urban northeast, midwest, and west between 1910 and 1970. Trout called Alabama Lutheran Bible Institute, "A kind of theological study center for black pastors." The school was, practically speaking, a high school in a one-room building on a college campus, with no academic links to the college.

Alabama Lutheran Bible Institute operated until 1954, when the Supreme Court issued the Brown v. Board of Education of Topeka decision. Racial segregation in public schools was ruled unconstitutional. Alabama Lutheran Bible Institute was a "separate educational facility" for Blacks operated by the American Lutheran Church. The Church, following lessons learned from the public square, closed the school, ending a chapter of separate and unequal education of Blacks by Lutherans. Fifty miles north of Montgomery, the Lutheran Synodical Conference of North America would continue segregating Black learners in Selma at Alabama Lutheran Academy and College (Concordia College). Blacks from the South were invited to enroll at American Lutheran Church colleges and seminaries, such as the Evangelical Lutheran Seminary in Columbus, Ohio, and Wittenburg University in Springfield, Ohio, following Brown v. Board of Education.

Nelson Trout brought an active Lutheran presence to the City of Montgomery through the parochial school of Trinity Lutheran Church, his work with the civil rights movement, and through a radio ministry on station WRMA. Trout left Montgomery in 1955, but not before befriending the Reverend Dr. Martin Luther King Jr., and Rosa Parks. While residing in Montgomery, Trout, and King were known to kid each other occasionally. Trout asked King how he got the name "Martin Luther." King replied by asking Trout how he came to be Lutheran. Trout joked that competition among Baptist preachers for placements was rough and that the Lutherans were begging for Negroes. Trout also remembered a visit from Rosa Parks. "I remember Rosa Parks coming to me one day asking if I would allow her to use our facility for NAACP youth. So at least once a month, Rosa Parks was in our congregation supervising the work of the young people sponsored by the NAACP."[14] The street address of Trinity Lutheran Church, Montgomery, is now Rosa L. Parks Avenue.

From Montgomery to Los Angeles

Nelson Trout became increasingly frustrated with life in Montgomery. Trout believed "his peers from the big Baptist and Methodist churches took neither Trinity nor its pastor seriously."[15] He was affected by racism in the late 1950s. In those years, Trout was clearly in a holding pattern: he was a new pastor wanting to be conscientious but discouraged by the immensity of the task. His dissatisfaction was evident:

> Having lived in Ohio all of my life, there was always things about the South that bothered me. I didn't understand the kind of discrimination that I saw in Alabama. Alabama was just something different. In other words it wasn't easy for me to learn how to step aside and let a white person walk down the sidewalk, you know. And I got tired of the perpetual grin on my face that was necessary in order to be accepted. So I was a little anxious about those kinds of things—riding in segregated transportation. I remember taking our daughter to Sears Roebuck store one day in Montgomery, and her insisting on going to the water fountain to get a drink of water, and there was a sign saying black and white, and how she insisted on drinking from the white fountain rather than the black fountain. When I got the call from Community Lutheran Church in Los Angeles, I knew that that was a call from God to get me out of that situation and I left Montgomery just at the beginning of the bus strike.[16]

Nelson Trout moved to Community Lutheran Church in Los Angeles, California, in 1955. Reverend Robert Graetz, the former intern and lay pastor of Community Lutheran Church moved to Trinity Lutheran, Montgomery, where he succeeded Nelson Trout as pastor. Graetz was the only white pastor to support the Montgomery Bus Boycott. Graetz and Trout were graduates of the Evangelical Lutheran Theological Seminary in Columbus, Ohio. A challenging ministry awaited Trout, also. African Americans began moving to Los Angeles in large numbers after 1900. For the next forty years, their numbers doubled every decade and by 1940 represented slightly more than 4 percent of the total population. Many Blacks moved into communities in South Los

Angeles through the 1950s and 1960s. Gradually through the 1950s, the southern section of Los Angeles, from Watts and west toward Inglewood and the Crenshaw District, became increasingly African American. This would be Trout's new home.

Other areas, such as West Adams, Leimert Park, and Baldwin Hills gradually became middle class and upper-middle class African American areas during this era. Sometimes referred as the "Second Great Migration" from the 1940s forward, African Americans migrated west. The Black population in Los Angeles leaped from 63,700 in 1940 to 763,000 in 1970. The influx of Blacks in Los Angeles eventually threatened the perceived property value for white homeowners. Right from the beginning of this period, the city was segregated because of racially restrictive housing covenants written into property deeds.[17] These covenants condensed the growing Black population to South Los Angeles and led to one of the most severe riots in the city's history, the 1965 Watts Riot. In Los Angeles, Trout's ministry was in a city with a clear demarcation of white America from Black America. It was a place where African Americans were as marginalized as anywhere in the South. Trout's ministry was among people who lived with a racial fault line, with white suburbs affluent in amenities, opportunity, and privilege cut off from the realities of poverty in the resource-deprived central city.[18] Trout served as pastor of Community Lutheran Church for seven years.

From Los Angeles to the Midwest

In 1962, the American Lutheran Church chose Trout as Associate Youth Director, a position which required a move to Minneapolis, Minnesota. Members of the Los Angeles congregation were not happy about him leaving. Losing a beloved pastor is painful, especially in a small congregation. Trout did not make his decision to leave casually. However painful it was for both pastor and congregation; Trout saw an opportunity to make the American Lutheran Church more inclusive. He said: "We've been banging on doors for a long time and that they are opening we dare not retreat." Conversely, the Reverend David Brown, ALC Youth Director, emphasized that Trout was sought for the position because of his abilities and not because of his race.[19] In this position,

Trout was the first African American to serve on the churchwide staff of the American Lutheran Church. Trout served as Associate Youth Director for four years.

In 1966, Grace Norwegian American Lutheran Congregation of Eau Claire, Wisconsin, invited Trout to serve as Associate Pastor. This invitation to serve in Eau Claire is noteworthy because it was uncommon for Black Lutheran pastors to be invited to minister in predominantly white Lutheran congregations. His pastoral service in Eau Claire offers a view of the inclusive vision that has long eluded Lutherans. While Trout does not say much about the call to Wisconsin, he remembered the short stay as "an interesting experience."[20]

> When I went to Eau Clair, Wisconsin, I remember the day we drove into town with my three kids in the back seat, and I remember my son saying, as we drove into town, "Daddy, look all of the houses are painted white." I think he was trying to tell me that he wasn't going to like it in Eau Claire. I can remember how we'd spend Sunday afternoon looking for black people. That was what we did for kicks on Sunday afternoon.[21]

Trout's education in the Lutheran academy equipped him to pastor a church in Eau Claire. However, in a setting where Swedes were the minority, navigating discussions on complicated issues such as biblical interpretation, liturgy, race, politics, or music presented new challenges. Some congregations and pastoral leaders can't bridge these divides. Stepping into a leadership role in a white Norwegian American Lutheran congregation in Wisconsin was challenging. The pastorate in Eau Claire was brief, lasting two years. Trout was preparing for a more significant role. He returned to the churchwide office of the American Lutheran Church in 1968 as Director of Urban Evangelism. He served in this position for two years.

In 1970, Trout was named executive director of Lutheran Social Services in Dayton, Ohio. His work as executive director involved the supervision of four departments of the Lutheran Social Service of the Miami Valley including Chaplaincy Service to eighteen public institutions in five counties (Montgomery, Miami, Preble, Butler, and Darke) and the Family and Children Services department serving unwed parents, adoptions, adoptive couples, counseling, and the distribution of material items in a "concrete services" program.

In 1975 Trout was employed as director of minority ministry studies at Lutheran Theological Seminary in Columbus, Ohio. Underrepresented minority students would have a special resource at the Seminary. Trout's job, in part, was to assist the seminary in attracting, nurturing, retaining, and graduating African Americans and other students of color on the campus and steer them to careers in the American Lutheran Church. He was also part of the teaching faculty. Trout was highly visible in the American Lutheran Church in this position. He traveled the country on behalf of the seminary as a recruiter, teacher, and preacher.

Trout's preaching style provided the overwhelming white Scandinavian denomination with a touch of passion more commonly associated with Black churches. Trout echoed the traditional flair of Black folk preaching, including rhetorical structures, vernacular language, antiphonal aspects, and hermeneutics, as seen in an essay published in *Lutheran Quarterly* in 1968:

> As I traveled about the country it appeared to me that the judgment of history is being executed in the streets of our cities. America is learning that you cannot violate God or neighbor with impunity. There is a biblical reference which says that "if one sows to the wind, [one] will reap the whirlwind." There is another which says, "The fathers have eaten grapes and have put their children's teeth on edge." The formidableness of such an inexorable justice is the nature of the challenge facing America, and I am fearful that we are not willing or ready to accept its decree.[22]

Many critical changes occurred in the United States in the late 1970s and early '80s. The conservative movement, New Right, experienced extraordinary growth during this time. It found interest among a diverse mixture of Americans, including evangelical Christians, anti-tax crusaders, advocates of deregulation and smaller markets, advocates of a more assertive American presence abroad, disaffected white liberals, and defenders of an unrestricted free market. Meanwhile at home, people watched family sitcoms like "The Cosby Show." In

1980, Robert L. Johnson launched the Black Entertainment Television (BET) network out of Washington, DC. In 1981, Val James of the Buffalo Sabres became the first Black American to play in the professional National Hockey League. In 1982, Bryant Gumbel became the anchor person of *The Today Show*, the first African American to claim the morning anchor post on a major television network. And in1983, Alice Walker's *The Color Purple* won the Pulitzer Prize for Fiction.

Pastor to Bishop

In 1983, Nelson Wesley Trout was elected bishop of the South Pacific District of the American Lutheran Church (ALC). At the time of his election, he was a professor and director of minority studies at Trinity Lutheran Seminary in Columbus. He was the first Black district bishop in the ALC and the first Black Lutheran bishop in the United States. At the time of Trout's election, the ALC had 2.3 million members who were primarily Scandinavian immigrants. It was one of the whitest denominations in the United States. In 1983, the South Pacific District had 144,000 members in 310 congregations in California, Nevada, Utah, Arizona, New Mexico, Hawaii, and some Texas counties. Trout was elected bishop on the third ballot at the district convention in Thousand Oaks, California, on June 17. He led throughout the voting, defeating the Reverend Cordon Selbo, pastor of St. Timothy Lutheran Church, San Jose, California by 389 votes to 308.

Two Black pastors served as part-time vice presidents in other Lutheran churches in the United States when Trout was elected a bishop. Will Herzfeld was vice president of the Association of Evangelical Lutheran Churches (AELC) and pastor of Bethlehem Lutheran Church, Oakland, California. Herzfeld served as AELC presiding bishop from 1984 through 1987. Joseph George Lavalais was the first African American to be elected a vice president of the Lutheran Church Missouri-Synod (LCMS) in 1981. Lavalais was the pastor of St. Philip Lutheran Church in Philadelphia.

Nelson Trout's tenure as a Lutheran bishop was three-and-a-half years. In 1987, Bishop Trout was defeated in his endeavor to become a bishop in the new Evangelical Lutheran Church in America (ELCA). Bishop Trout was defeated by the Reverend J. Roger Anderson, a

Southern California regional official for the Lutheran Church in America (LCA), during a vote at the constituting convention of the ELCA's Southern California West Synod on June 5. The vote was 103 to 196. Trout believed he was defeated because of his political views and unapologetic stance on liberation theology.

Legacy

Trout was awarded an Honorary Doctor of Divinity degree by Wartburg College, Waverly, Iowa, in 1970. In 1984 he was awarded an Honorary Doctor of Humane Letters by California Lutheran University, Thousand Oaks, California. In 1991, Trout's alma mater, Trinity Lutheran Seminary, established the Nelson W. Trout Lectureship in Preaching to honor his life and legacy. Nelson Trout died in Inglewood, California, on September 20, 1996 at the age of 77. He is commemorated in the Calendar of Saints of the Evangelical Lutheran Church in America on September 20.

Notes

1. *Urbancrest Homecoming* (1996). African America Civic Leaders Reunions. Book made for the 106th anniversary of the incorporation of Urbancrest. Digital-collections.columbuslibrary.org/digital/collection/African/id/26820. Retrieved January 12, 2022.
2. Carl F. Reuss. *Interview with Nelson Trout.* Oral History Collection of the American Lutheran Church, Evangelical Lutheran Church in America, the Lutheran Church in America, ELCA Archives, 1986, p. 41.
3. Nelson Trout—ELCA Archives Bio file 1.dpf, 40.
4. Nelson Trout—ELCA Archives Bio file 1.dpf, 40.
5. Ndanganeni Phaswana. "A Lutheran Bishop's Apartheid Memoir." *Lutheran Forum* (Fall 2013).
6. Nelson Trout—ELCA Archives Bio file 1.dpf, 42.
7. "Who We Are." https://www.reconcilingworks.org/about/. Retrieved, March 22, 2023.
8. Taylor Branch. *Parting the Waters: America in the King Years 1954–63* (New York. Simon and Schuster, 1988), 125.

9. Pedrito Maynard-Reid, *Diverse Worship: African-American, Caribbean, and Hispanic Perspectives* (Downers Grove, IL: Inter Varsity Press, 2000), 61.
10. Melva Wilson Costen, *African-American Christian Worship* (Nashville: Abingdon Press, 1993), 20.
11. Jeremy Gray. "The execution of Jeremiah Reeves: Alabama teen's death sentence helped drive civil rights movement." February 4, 2015, https://www.al.com/news/2015/02/the_execution_of_jeremiah_reev.html. Retrieved August 5, 2022.
12. Christopher F. Drewes, *Half a Century of Lutheranism among Our Colored People: A Jubilee Book* (St. Louis: Concordia Publishing House, 1927), 15.
13. *Minutes*, Joint Synod of Ohio, 1924, Region 1 Archives of the Evangelical Lutheran Church in America, Record group, Evangelical Lutheran Joint Synod of Ohio Records, p. 47. Retrieved from https://archives.plu.edu/index.php/region-1-archives-of-the-evangelical-lutheran-church-in-america
14. Reuss, *Interview with Nelson Trout*, 11.
15. Branch, *Parting the Waters*, 125.
16. Reuss, *Interview with Nelson Trout*, 12.
17. Mike Sonksen. "The History of South Central Los Angeles and its Struggle with Gentrification," PBS SoCal KCET (2017). https://www.kcet.org/shows/city-rising/the-history-of-south-central-los-angeles-and-its-struggle-with-gentrification. Retrieved August 6, 2022.
18. Andrea Gibbons. *City of Segregation: One Hundred Years of Struggle for Housing in Los Angeles*. (Brooklyn, NY: Verso Books, 2018), 122.
19. "First Negro Clergyman Named to ALC Headquarters Staff." *Religious News Service*, September 28, 1962, p. 2.
20. "First Negro Clergyman Named to ALC Headquarters Staff," 13
21. "First Negro Clergyman Named to ALC Headquarters Staff," 13
22. Nelson Trout, *The Lutheran Quarterly* (May 1968).

CHAPTER 7

Will Herzfeld

Presiding Bishop of the Association of Evangelical Lutheran Churches

WILL HERZFELD WAS a prominent leader serving as president or vice president of several organizations involved in advocacy and reconciliation? His life chronicles a slice of racism in the church and American life, yet he responded by getting involved.

Early Life and Education

Willie Lawrence (Will) Herzfeld grew up in the Jim Crow South. He was born on the Frazier Farm in Greensboro, Alabama, on June 9, 1937. Herzfeld, whose great-grandfather was German, was introduced to the Lutheran church when his Baptist grandmother enrolled him and his two younger siblings in a Lutheran school.[1] The Herzfeld family were founding members of Faith Lutheran Church in Mobile, Alabama, and Mount Calvary Lutheran Church in Tilden, Alabama. Will was a son of Julius Herzfeld Sr. and Nettie Frazier Herzfeld. Will took delight in the diversity of his heritage and was always quick to point humorously to his German ancestry. His first marriage was to Thressa M. Alston in Kannapolis, North Carolina, on June 11, 1961. The couple had four children—two daughters and two sons—three of whom lived to adulthood. Their first child, a daughter, lived only one day. Will's second wife, the Reverend Michele L. Robinson, pastored United in Christ Lutheran Church in Chicago. Michele died in May 2001.

Will's parents enrolled him in the parochial elementary school sponsored by Faith Lutheran Church, where his family and members of Faith Church nurtured his Christian identity. He completed his high school education at Alabama Lutheran Academy in Selma. The school in Selma was founded through the work of Rosa J. Young and the mission developers of the Lutheran Synodical Conference of North America. Alabama Lutheran Academy filtered its curriculum through a religious lens.

After graduating with an associate of arts degree in 1957 from Immanuel Lutheran College in Greensboro, North Carolina, Will was awarded a master of divinity in 1961 at Immanuel Lutheran Seminary. Launched at Concord, North Carolina, in 1903 by the Mission Board of the Evangelical Lutheran Synodical Conference of North America "for Mission work among the Heathen and the Negro", Immanuel College and Seminary's mission was to prepare African Americans seeking professional status as pastors or teachers in Black congregations of the Lutheran Synodical Conference.[2] The reference to mission work among "the Heathen and the Negro" represents a colonial-era Church understanding of mission work.[3] In 1905, the school was relocated to Greensboro, North Carolina, across the street from North Carolina Agricultural and Technical College. While well intended, the education offered to Will as a student was inferior in quantity and quality. A Study Commission appointed by the 1958 Synodical Conference Convention concluded:

> Plants, salary schedules, libraries, and general conditions at Greensboro and Selma make it extremely difficult to understand how the staff of these institutions could work with pleasure to themselves and profit to their students through the years. Both institutions stand as dismal monuments to the neglect, lack of vision, and stepchild approach of the supporting synods in the area of Negro education.[4]

The educational experiences at Alabama Lutheran Academy did not slow or dim Will's quest for learning. He completed post-graduate studies at Concordia Seminary in St. Louis, Missouri, and at the University of Alabama in Tuscaloosa. He held an honorary doctor of divinity degrees from Christ Seminary-Seminex, St. Louis, and the Center for Urban Black Studies, Graduate Theological Union, Berkeley, California. In 1977, the Lutheran School of Theology at Chicago (LSTC), one of the seven ELCA seminaries, gave him a Distinguished Alumni Award. Christ Seminary merged with LSTC in 1987.

Ordination and Pastoral Work

Ordained by the Lutheran Church—Missouri Synod in 1961, Will brought an unusual display of verbal, pragmatic, leadership, and cognitive skills to the church. Will's first assignment after seminary was in the Southern District of the Lutheran Church—Missouri Synod. Will was pastor at Christ Lutheran Church Tuscaloosa, Alabama (1961–1965). Organized as a congregation of the American Lutheran Church in 1947, the church was an expansion of a school organized in 1917. The American Lutheran Church's mission strategy in Alabama and Mississippi was to begin first with a school, "and then the school would be the basis for the establishment of a congregation."[5] At Christ Lutheran Church, the model was a success. In 1954, when the United States Supreme Court issued Brown vs. Board of Education, the American Lutheran Church essentially abandoned "Negro Mission work," transferring three congregations to the Missouri Synod: Trinity (now United) in Montgomery, Christ Tuscaloosa, and St. Paul in Birmingham. Maintaining a dual system for mission work was costly for the American Lutheran Church, and comparatively speaking, the Synodical Conference was more productive on the same territory. The Missouri Synod and the Lutheran Synodical Conference of North America have been successfully involved in the Alabama Black Belt region since 1916. By 1927, twenty-nine Black Lutheran congregations and preaching points were in the area as well as twenty-seven day schools. During this period, Wilcox County was the fastest-growing area of Lutheranism in the United States.[6] As a result of this mission work, as many as twenty-four African American Lutheran churches were formed, including congregations in Mobile (1920), Atmore (1925), Montrose (1930), Point Clear (1951), and Pritchard (1954). This is the Alabama in which Will Herzfeld began his career.

Leadership

While serving at Christ Church, Will, working with the Reverend T.Y. Rogers of First African Baptist Church and others, organized the local chapter of the Southern Christian Leadership Conference (SCLC) and was its first president. At the forefront of the civil rights movement in

Tuscaloosa, the chapter organized a march on June 9, 1964, to advocate for integrating restrooms and water fountains in the new Tuscaloosa County Courthouse. Will walked with community members attempting to protest segregated drinking fountains and toilets in the county courthouse. On a day remembered as "Bloody Tuesday," police and a mob of white people attacked and beat the marchers. Dozens of protestors received medical care due to injuries inflicted by the mob, and police jailed nearly a hundred more.[7]

Will was also President of the Alabama State SCLC. In 1966, the Tuscaloosa Businessmen's League honored him as an Outstanding Citizen. He received three Service to Youth awards from the Benjamin Barnes branch of the Young Men's Christian Association (YMCA) in Tuscaloosa. His involvement in the SCLC led to his association with the Reverend Dr. Martin Luther King Jr. While pastoring in Tuscaloosa, Will also served the LCMS Southern District in several leadership roles.

From 1964 to 1966, Will was vice president of the Lutheran Human Relations Association of America (LHRAA). Founded in 1953, the organization worked to improve race relations in the church and advance the civil rights movement. The mission of LHRAA complimented Will's work in Tuscaloosa. LHRAA provided members with theological grounding for social engagement and so much more. The founder of LHRAA, the Reverend Andrew Schulze, believed that the solid Christological nature of Lutheranism, with its emphasis on Christ and the saving grace of Christ, supported an involved Christian witness.[8] Will had a strong moral compass and was motivated by solidarity with the people he lived with in his neighborhood. In the spirit of LHRAA, Will placed himself alongside the communities he served, speaking and acting on political and social issues. Will's understanding of Lutheran theology called for Christian social responsibility and public action.

Although ordained for pastoral ministry in a congregation, Will wore several leadership hats beyond congregations. For Black Lutheran pastors, this was not unusual. The limited number of Black pastors serving in the Lutheran Church in the United States were scattered in many directions, making their presence seem almost virtual. While serving as vice president of the Lutheran Human Relations Association of America, he was, from 1965 to 1973, urban minister in the Lutheran—Missouri Synod's California–Nevada–Hawaii

District. The relocation from Tuscaloosa to Oakland, California, was more than a two-hour time difference. While issues in Tuscaloosa were often related to the racial Black/white binary, the California–Nevada–Hawaii District was one of the most culturally diverse locations in the Lutheran Church—Missouri Synod. Will's work in the district placed him in the company of a medley of people, including Indigenous people, brown people, LGBTQIA+ people, mixed-race people, and migrant communities—individuals who did not find themselves within the dominant Black/white narrative. Part of Will's role in the district was bringing people together, sharing the gospel, and creating community. The Lutheran Synodical Conference sought to prepare African Americans seeking professional status as pastors or teachers in Black congregations of the Conference. Job descriptions, experience, and opportunities changed the itinerary the Synodical Conference established for Will.

In 1973, Bethlehem Lutheran Church and School in Oakland invited Will to be pastor. Bethlehem was a predominantly African American congregation founded in 1929 when five Black Lutheran women, originally from Louisiana, organized the Lutheran Witness of West Oakland.[9] The congregation was listed in 1934 by the Lutheran Church—Missouri Synod as Bethlehem Colored Mission.[10] Bethlehem's building was formerly the German Evangelical Lutheran Zion Church (later Zion Lutheran Church) and dates back to February 19, 1882. Bethlehem remained a congregation of the LCMS until 1975 when it was one of the first to break away from the Lutheran Church—Missouri Synod and join the Association of Evangelical Lutheran Churches (AELC). The AELC resulted from a break in 1976 from the Lutheran Church—Missouri Synod in a dispute over the authority and interpretation of Scripture.[11] In 1976, Will assumed the post of vice president of AELC.

In 1984, Will was elected presiding bishop of the Association of Evangelical Lutheran Churches. He was the first African American to serve as presiding bishop and chief pastor of a Lutheran church body in the United States. Simultaneously, Will was a member of the Commission for a New Lutheran Church. The ELCA was constituted in 1987 and began operation in 1988 as a result of the union of the American Lutheran Church (ALC), the Lutheran Church in America (LCA), and the Association of Evangelical Lutheran Churches

(AELC).[12] Will played a crucial role in the seventy-member commission, which drafted the constitution and other agreements. Will was a strong voice for "representational principles." Some in the ELCA greeted these principles with criticism. Robert Benne, an ELCA theologian, labeled the principals as quotas.[13] Some experienced white male pastors and a few white theologians opposed the principles that called for inclusiveness. The principles required that every committee, task force, and assembly in the new church had to be 60 percent lay, 40 percent clergy, 50 percent women, and 10 percent either persons of color or people whose primary language is other than English; the council acted to increase that representation to at least 25 percent.[14] Will championed these principles.

Will remained pastor of Bethlehem while serving as bishop of the AELC. In December 1992, Will became Director of Global Community and Overseas Operations of the Division for Global Mission/ELCA, located in Chicago, Illinois. In this role, Will was the ELCA's primary representative overseas. His work with the Division for Global Mission/ELCA involved contacts with more than eighty companion churches. Will shared in facilitation conversations addressing and finding solutions to the root causes of poverty. He was part of the ELCA's efforts in combating diseases like malaria and HIV/AIDS in fourteen African countries, including Malawi. In 2002, Will visited the Central African Republic. He attended the ordination of Rachel Doumbaye, the first woman Lutheran pastor in that country. While in the Central African Republic, he contracted cerebral malaria. A month later, on May 9, Will Herzfeld died at Resurrection Medical Center, Chicago. He was 64 years old.

Legacy

Will's life shows how one individual can artfully, sometimes angrily, and resourcefully responded to racism in the church and American life. Will succeeded in formal learning in the American Lutheran education system despite subpar schooling in parochial schools in Alabama and at Immanuel Lutheran Seminary in North Carolina. He was a tireless witness and worker for justice in the world. He was a bridge builder. To bring about healing in human relations, Will worked for reconciliation and cooperation in the church at home and between global churches. He was a witness to the faith he had in God and God's reconciling action through the good news of Jesus Christ.

Notes

1. "Rev. Will L. Herzfeld, 64," *Chicago Tribune.*" https://www.chicagotribune.com/news/ct-xpm-2002-05-12-0205120212-story.html. Retrieved, September 2, 2022.
2. Christopher Drewes, *Half a Century of Lutheranism among Our Colored People* (St. Louis, Concordia Publishing House), 86.
3. Carter G. Woodson, *The History of the Negro Church* (Washington, DC: Associated Press, 1923), 2.
4. Richard C. Dickinson, *Roses and Thorns: The Centennial Edition of Black Lutheran Mission and Ministry in the Lutheran Church—Missouri Synod.* (St. Louis: Concordia Publishing House, 1977), 165.
5. Carl F. Reuss. *Interview with Nelson Trout.* Oral History Collection of the American Lutheran Church, Association of Evangelical Lutheran Churches, The Lutheran Church in America, (Evangelical Lutheran Church in America Archives, 1986), 6.
6. Mark Granquist, "The Mother of Black Lutheranism in America." *Living Lutheran* February 4, 2021).
7 "Tuscaloosa's Bloody Tuesday." *The Tuscaloosa News.* February 21, 2009.
8. Kathryn Galchutt. *The Career of Andrew Schulze, 1924—1968: Lutherans and Race in the Civil Rights Era* (Macon: Mercer University Press, 2005).
9. "Who We Are," Bethlehem Lutheran Church, Oakland, California. https://blcoakblog.wordpress.com/who-we-are/. Retrieved March 28, 2023.
10. "Bethlehem Lutheran Church," https://localwiki.org/oakland/Bethlehem_Lutheran_Church. Retrieved March 29, 2023.
11. James C. Burkee, *Power, Politics, and the Missouri Synod* (Minneapolis, Fortress Press: 2013).
12. Edgar R. Trexler, *Anatomy of a Merger: People, Dynamics, and Decisions That Shaped the ELCA Minneapolis* (Augsburg Fortress, 1992).
13. Robert Benne, "The Trials of American Lutheranism." *First Things* (May 2011). https://www.firstthings.com/article/2011/05/the-trials-of-american-lutheranism
14. ELCA Constitution 5.01.e., 5.01.F19., and 5.01.H21.

CHAPTER 8

William Griffin

Lutheran Pastor in Montgomery Involved in the Civil Rights Movement

WILLIE AND BESSIE Griffin, parents of fourteen children, were determined for their children to succeed. They encouraged their son to attend Immanuel College, and he did not disappoint them. Bill exceeded their expectations and became an influential pastor and teacher. He instilled the "Ora et Labora" work ethic in his children. William used his work ethic to serve as a pastor and be involved in activism and advocacy.

Early Life and Education

William "Bill" Griffin was a pastor in the Lutheran Church—Missouri Synod. Griffin, born in 1929 in Kannapolis, North Carolina, has roots in the Lutheran Church in the United States. His grandmother, Margaret Steward Crowell Griffin, was a member of Mount Calvary Lutheran Church in Kannapolis in the 1890s. Willie and Bessie Griffin, Bill's parents, were also members of Mount Calvary. Bill was the third of the fourteen children. Bill remembers a plaque on the wall in his parent's house with the words "Ora et Labora'"—pray and work. The expression, frequently linked to the Rule of Benedict, underscores the significance of prayer and physical work in attaining spiritual progress. His parents emphasized the importance of both work and strong faith in God.[1]

Owing to Jim Crow segregation, Black schools in North Carolina were under-resourced during Bill's early years.[2] While the Black community welcomed Lutheran schools, they too were underfunded. Small tuition amounts and modest contributions from small Black congregations supported the schools. But the Lutheran schools had an important distinction. Lutheran schools nurtured the spiritual growth of children. Teachers began class with prayer and taught kindness from the example of Jesus. These lessons were necessary to Willie and Bessie Griffin. In 1933, Bill enrolled in Mount Calvary parochial school in Kannapolis. However, he transferred to George Washington Carver High School since the Lutheran school offered only elementary grades. George Washington Carver High School was opened for Black students originally in 1923 as Centerville Colored School. Graduating as the top-ranked student in the class of 1945, Bill earned the distinction of valedictorian. At the urging of his parents, Bill entered Immanuel Lutheran College in Greensboro, North Carolina. "My parents were the major decision-makers. College was the only way out for us,"[3] he writes. While College education was not the only route to success, the Griffin family valued it as their children's shortest pathway to upward mobility. Supporting a large family was challenging for Willie Griffin, who experienced stress and depressive episodes. Yet, he wanted his children to have a better quality of life than he and Bessie had, and they worked hard to provide for them. He wanted education for each of his fourteen children. The elder Griffins selected Immanuel Lutheran College for Bill because it was the best place to go for the dollars. The African Methodist Episcopal Church's Livingstone College in Salisbury, North Carolina, was closer and offered Bill a scholarship, but he got a better offer from Immanuel. The elder Griffins shopped for the best financial deal.[4]

Entering college was a transformative experience for Bill. He had been valedictorian of his high school class. Some of Bill's learning peers were also valedictorians of their classes. He mused that they would have been valedictorians of his graduating class at George Washington Garver High School. He entered classrooms with students who had gone to better schools, he thought. Students came to Immanuel from the southern, southeastern, and eastern states. "There were people from all over the East Coast who had finished much better high schools than I had experienced."[5] Bill met his spouse, Ella Coleman, at Emmanuel. Ella was from Far Rockaway, Queens, New York. Immanuel broadened Bill's perspective. He engaged the challenges before him. His first-year class, while diverse, was not more than thirty students.[6]

Immanuel Lutheran College

The Lutheran Synodical Conference of North America launched Immanuel Lutheran College in Concord, North Carolina, on March 2, 1903.[7] In 1904, the Synodical Conference voted to require African Americans seeking professional status as pastors or teachers to enroll there.

Lutherans in the United States began a dual system of higher education. In September 1905, the Synodical Conference moved Immanuel College to Greensboro, North Carolina. Although Immanuel had a high school department, a junior college, and a seminary, student enrollment was low. From its founding in 1904 to its closing in 1961, yearly enrollment was never above a hundred and fifty students. The final graduating class numbered nine from the high school and thirteen from the college. Griffin described the school as a small family.

The racial makeup of the faculty at Immanuel College, or any other educational institution, should ideally reflect student enrollment and the wider community. It is concerning that the faculty at Immanuel was primarily white, when it was founded to provide educational

Image 8.1. Lutheran College, Colored, Greensboro, NC.

Source: Durwood Barbour Collection of North Carolina Postcards (P077), North Carolina Collection Photographic Archives, Wilson Library, UNC-Chapel Hill.

opportunities for Black Americans excluded from white Lutheran colleges. In Bill's final year, Rev. O. R. L. Lynn, an African American, was added to the faculty.

Bill Griffin's perspective on education at a largely overlooked historically Black Lutheran College in the United States provides valuable insights into the experiences of students and faculty members at Immanuel.[8] "I found the studies [at Immanuel] challenging." In addition to general education requirements mandated by the State of North Carolina, there was a particular emphasis on theology, and students were required to study Latin and German. Overall, Bill saw the challenging nature of studies at Immanuel as a positive educational experience.[9]

While Bill viewed parts of learning as a positive experience, his reflections on the professors were less affirming." The professors, I think were a lot more paternalistic than they should have been towards us." To Bill, the professors were demeaning and patronizing. "They thought that we were not going to amount to very much." William H. Kampschmidt, president of Immanuel from 1951–1961, offered a view of Blacks in the profession Bill aspired to:

> Many of the preachers and teachers of the negro race are the leaders and guides of their people, but thousands of these are there only to live a lazy, frivolous, and often despicable life, making a sham of their profession and are a disgrace to their Lord and His Church.[10]

Kampschmidt's sentiments are condescending and problematic to students who doubtless had uncles, brothers, friends, and other relatives who were Black preachers. Bill lamented, "Most of the professors at Immanuel probably would not have been teaching at the colleges and seminaries of the Lutheran Church—Missouri Synod. They would not have been able to cut the mustard there."[11] While Bill identifies Immanuel as a school of the Lutheran Church—Missouri Synod, the school was operated by the Lutheran Synodical Conference of North America. Founded in 1872, the membership of the Conference fluctuated as various synods joined and left it. The Conference membership responsible for Immanuel included the Wisconsin Evangelical Lutheran Synod, the Evangelical Lutheran Synod (Norwegian), the Synod of

Evangelical Churches (Slovak), and the Lutheran Church—Missouri Synod.

Among Griffin's recollections of Immanuel was that the school, while not isolated geographically, stood alone in another way. Immanuel students had access to North Carolina Agricultural and Technical State College and Bennett College. Both were in Greensboro. Contacts between students at Immanuel and those schools were generally social. "I did not know a lot about the other educational institutions around. They were just not significant to my experience. We had a handle on the truth over there." Immanuel was, functionally, an organizational silo where students were largely unaware of the larger environment.

Bill made a special visit to A&T State College to hear a lecture. "It was the first time we had ever gone to that school, which was six blocks away." The lecturer was Dr. Osmund Smallwood, chairman of the English Department at Ohio State University and a graduate of Immanuel Seminary. Bill wasn't impressed with Smallwood's lecture. Bill was expecting Smallwood to share the gospel during the sessions and was disappointed when Smallwood did not. The dean of Immanuel, Dr. Lynn, relayed Bill's critique to Dr. Smallwood. Smallwood replied, "If this is the kind of students you have, I pity you." Years later, Bill admitted that Smallwood was right in his assessment. "We thought we were the center of the universe. By our judgment, Bennett College and A&T College weren't good schools. We had the truth."[12] Bill's assessment of Bennett College and A&T State College was no doubt influenced by the stated mission of Immanuel College: "To reach and proclaim the word of God in all its truths and purity."[13]

Griffin believed that white Lutherans had a specific aim in opening schools like Immanuel. The primary purpose of these schools was not simply to provide education but rather to "Christianize" African Americans according to Lutheran doctrines about Christianity. It is worth noting that this belief is shaped by historical context. During slavery and segregation in the United States, many white Christian denominations saw their missionary work among African Americans as a way to "civilize" and "uplift" them. This involved promoting Christianity to "save" African Americans from their supposed "heathen" beliefs and practices.

Secondly, Bill believed that the historical context of segregation and discrimination in the United States that resulted in establishing separate educational institutions for Black and white students was also a practice of Lutherans. This was particularly true in the South, where the law enforced segregation until the mid-twentieth century. Immanuel College functionally kept the pressure off white Lutheran colleges to enroll African Americans. African Americans who applied for admission were steered to Immanuel College.[14]

Griffin also remembers role models and the life-long friends he met at Immanuel. The dean of students, Rev. R. O. L. Lynn, was a Black role model. He attended the University of Chicago and received a BA in the 1930s. Lynn was a first lieutenant in the army during World War I. On November 13, 1922, fifty-nine years after Daniel Payne became the first Black American college president, Dr. Robert Otho L. Lynn was installed as president of Alabama Lutheran Academy and College. He was the first Black American to lead a Lutheran college in the United States.[15] Lutherans in the United States would not entrust the college president role to another Black American for an extended period.[16] The Synodical Conference determined that a Black teacher would better understand the racial characteristics, ideas, objectives, and peculiarities of their race, as they discussed reasons for establishing Immanuel. However, despite this conclusion, the school was initially staffed with an all-white faculty.[17]

Pastoral Work

In 1951, William Griffin was the sole student in his graduating class upon completing his studies at Immanuel Seminary. His first ministry assignment was in Wilcox County, Alabama. He served at Holy Cross, Camden; Our Savior, Possum Bend; and Redeemer, Long Mile. He preached at all three churches every Sunday and, with Rev. Richard Dickerson, recorded sermons for a radio station in Monroeville. He writes,

> God, and I tributed this to Him, put me in Alabama, out in Wilcox County, with some fine people who helped me develop into whatever kind of pastor I finally became. The Clarks, out in Long Mile, the Bodleys in Possum Bend, and the Hardys in Camden are just a few names that come to mind. These people took my wife and me under their wing as their children

> and really guided us along the way. I owe a debt of gratitude to these people. That's really where I learned what it is to be a pastor from these people. Seminaries can't teach that![18]

Bill's energy, passion, and preaching skill earned attention, and he was invited in 1952 to serve as pastor of Trinity Lutheran Church, Selma, where Rosa Young was a member. Rosa became godmother to his son. In 1954, Griffin accepted a call to develop a new mission congregation in Montgomery, Alabama. Grace Lutheran Church was two blocks from Dexter Avenue Baptist Church, where Dr. Martin Luther King Jr. was pastor. The congregation was also two blocks from First Baptist Church, where Rev. Ralph David Abernathy was pastor.

When the Griffins wanted new draperies for their new home in Montgomery, they hired a local seamstress whose name was Rosa Parks. When Martin Luther King Jr. called local pastors to begin the Montgomery Bus Boycott, Griffin got one of those calls. During the bus boycott, Griffin used his 1954 Chevrolet to offer transportation for individuals to get to their jobs. It is not widely known that Bill was one of the early Lutheran pastors in Montgomery to participate in the civil rights movement.

Montgomery to Chicago

In 1956, Christ the King Lutheran Church in Chicago invited Bill to assume the role of pastor. In Chicago, Griffin worked with others to form the Kenwood–Oakland Community Organization (KOCO). The mission of Kenwood-Oakland included shaping campaigns that increased the resources and services available to families and residents of the North Kenwood and Oakland communities. In 1968, when Martin Luther King Jr. was assassinated, street demonstrations erupted in Chicago, resulting in the deaths of eleven people.[19] Bill and other Black Lutheran pastors met to discuss ways to assist in a time of crisis and to help whites in the church better respond to the needs of their Black neighbors. The result was the establishment of the Black Lutheran Clergy Caucus.

Bill also taught at Concordia University in River Forest, Illinois, and Concordia Seminary in St. Louis, Missouri. Bill earned a master's degree in education from Concordia University and was awarded an honorary doctorate from Concordia Seminary. Bill served at two additional Chicago churches in Chicago's South Side before "retiring" in 1983.

After retirement, he continued in various capacities for another fifteen years with Lutheran churches, district offices, and agencies as: a staff person for the LCMS Northern Illinois District; a mission facilitator; director of an anti-racism project; interim pastor for Our Savior Lutheran Church in Orlando, Florida; chaplain assistant to the dean and religion instructor at Luther High School South in Chicago; as area representative for Wheat Ridge Ministries; and as vacancy pastor for Zion Lutheran Church in Chicago. In 2009, Reverend Griffin retired a second time to care for his wife, Ella Mae, who died in February 2015. Two of Bill and Ella Mae's sons, Marvin and Mark, followed his path and became Lutheran pastors. A daughter, Marie, administered a nonprofit serving people experiencing poverty in Pension Town, New Orleans. She married a Lutheran pastor.

Notes

1. "The 'Curtain Call,' Civil Rights from Alabama to Chicago: A Lutheran Pastor Reflects." *Timeline Newsletter* (Spring 2019): 4. Griffin entered a Lutheran parochial school in Kannapolis around 1933/34. https://files.lcms.org/file/preview/uo7SBDHUqzuTcg55sIarQUhKvC6uZcrz. Retrieved October 26, 2022.
2. Valinda W. Littlefield, "A Yearly Contract with Everybody and His Brother: Durham County, North Carolina Black Female Public School Teachers, 1885–1927," *Journal of Negro History* 79, no. 1, 43–44.
3. James R. Thomas. *African American Education in the Context of Lutheran Collegiate Institutions Since the Late Nineteenth Century*. Unpublished Doctoral Dissertation, University of Minnesota (1998), 142.
4. Thomas, *African American Education*, 143.
5. Thomas, *African American Education*, 142.
6. Thomas, *African American Education*, 142.
7. W. H. Kampschmidt. "Why the Evangelical Lutheran Church Established and Maintains a College for Negroes?" *Journal of Negro Education*, 29, no. 3 (Summer, 1960): 299–306.
8. NCPEDIA omits Immanuel Lutheran College in a list of North Carolina historically black colleges. North Carolina has twelve historically Black

colleges and universities. Ten of these schools continue to operate today. https://www.ncpedia.org/education/hbcu. Retrieved April 10, 2023.

9. Immanuel Lutheran College, Catalog. The Library at the University of North Carolina at Chapel Hill. The Collection of North Carolina. http://archive.org/details/catalogueofimman19271928imma/mode/2up?view=theater. Retrieved April 6, 2023.
10. Kampschmidt, "Why the Evangelical Lutheran Church Established and Maintains a College for Negroes?" 303.
11. Thomas, *African American Education*, 143.
12. Thomas, *African American Education*, 145.
13. Kampschmidt, "Why the Evangelical Lutheran Church Established and Maintains a College for Negroes?" 305.
14. Thomas, *African American Education*, 147.
15. Thomas, *African American Education*, 147–148.
16. It would be 74 years before another Black American would lead a Lutheran school of higher education. On November 9, 1997, Dr. James Kenneth Echols was installed as president of the Lutheran School of Theology in Chicago.
17. Kampschmidt, "Why the Evangelical Lutheran Church Established and Maintains a College for Negroes?" 301.
18. Thomas, *African American Education*, 151.
19. "Chicago Has a Long History of Civil Unrest." CBS News. https://www.cbsnews.com/chicago/news/chicago-has-long-history-of-civil-unrest-but-downtown-location-makes-this-year-different/. Retrieved November 2, 2022.

CHAPTER 9

Albert Pero Jr.

Black Theologian and Tenured Professor at a Lutheran Seminary

WHEN WILLIAM GRIFFIN was a student at Immanuel Seminary in Greensboro, North Carolina, he met a young scholar on the path to becoming the first Black professional theologian and tenured professor at a Lutheran seminary in the United States.

Early Life and Education

Albert "Pete" Pero Jr. was the first Lutheran in his family. Pete's introduction to Lutheranism occurred when he met students from Concordia Seminary in his St. Louis neighborhood. The students invited Pete to worship at a Lutheran congregation. His parents were not afraid of Pete worshipping in other churches. Pete's parents encouraged him to accept the invitation. The Peros believed that joining church could facilitate Pete's transition into the wider world, enabling him to succeed. "They decided for me. That was crystal clear. Also, our family, along with a pile of other folks, were highly religious Christian people way before we knew anything about Lutheranism. So, Lutheranism as a Christian religious system, I guess, kind of helped us articulate and conceptualize some of the things."[1] Pero's mother, Archie, became a Lutheran soon after Pete. His father, Albert Pero Sr., remained a member of an African American congregation, First Baptist Church in St. Louis. Predominantly Black places of worship held a considerable presence in the lives of Black Americans when Pete was rising to maturity. Most African Americans in the United States are followers of Christianity, and many practice their faith with great devotion according to traditional belief criteria.

The Pero family migrated north from South Carolina and Louisiana. They were pious people, and he described the family as one "heavy into religion." Pete learned Bible stories from his grandmother. She taught using a flannel board on Saturday nights.[2] Pete's home and family ties were strengthened by emotional and psychological support from his parents and grandmother. Pete learned to feel good about himself at home.

Pete attended the segregated public schools of St. Louis. He graduated from Vashon High School in South St. Louis. When it opened in 1927, Vashon was the second high school for Black students in St. Louis. Teachers counseled him to enter the medical profession. The teachers at Vashon High School showed a keen interest in Pete and encouraged him to strive for more. While Pero maintained an interest in science for the rest of his life, he was on another mission.

St. Paul's Lutheran Academy and College

In fall 1953, Pete entered St. Paul's Lutheran Academy and College in Concordia, Missouri. Pete arrived at St. Paul's a stranger among students who belonged in many ways to a family. The Lutheran Church—Missouri Synod was like a big family. Linked by family names, attendance at parochial grade and high schools, and graduation from LCMS colleges, families in the Synod were close. Before enrolling at Concordia white students in large numbers were from Lutheran congregations and attended Lutheran elementary and high schools. Pero's recollections of his first two years in a Lutheran school are laced with humor and pointed critique of his experiences with the locals in Concordia, Missouri:

> When I first went to St. Paul's Academy, I had to leave town literally by sundown. I would go in there and grab something at the drugstore, or something like that, but I could not stay in that town after sundown. I went through the entire years there unable to get a haircut, and ultimately, the students forced the barber to come on campus to cut my hair. So that was during a period of time when it was getting kind of rough to co-exist with another culture.[3]

Pete's reference to "sundown" calls to mind the experiences of many Black college students attending school in all-white communities where Black people and other minorities avoided public places after sundown. Many all-white American towns forbade Black people from being within the city limits after nightfall. For example, a sign that hung outside of Siloam Springs (Benton County), Arkansas, well into the 1960s claimed "Healing Waters, Beautiful Parks, Many Springs, Public Library," alongside another sign: "No Malaria, No Mosquitoes, and No Negroes."[4] These roadside signs greeted Black students at Siloam Springs College and John Brown University. Concordia, Missouri was similar to Siloam Springs, Arkansas, being a "sundown town," according to Pete.

Pete described his time at St. Paul's Academy and College as "being caught up in a sea of whiteness." Pete experienced being one of just a few Black faces in a predominantly white environment. This came with challenges:

> I went to school with a pile of folks infected with a peculiar European gene-fill, commonly known as whiteness. I was surrounded by the white community, and I was the only black person around there. After that, I think one black student drifted in after another. But really, not many more than one at a time.[5]

Pete was affected by the near absence of diversity among students and faculty of color at the St. Paul's campus. This created a sense of disconnection for him. Racial segregation in neighborhoods, schools, and churches perpetuates anti-Black prejudice in the United States, resulting in many white students arriving on college campuses without ever having had meaningful interactions with their Black peers. The result is that Black students, introduced to majority-white campuses long before diversity and inclusion initiatives were raised, had no scaffolding or effective support systems in their campus environment. Daniel Black has written about Black parents who shipped their children to college "in hostile white territory" to get a superior education.[6] He argues that historically Black colleges and universities are just as effective as predominantly white institutions in fostering higher learning without the stress and social isolation like Pete experienced.[7]

Despite social isolation, Pete's academic experience was rigorous at St. Paul's. The biggest challenges for Pete were languages and confessional theology. He had no prior exposure to language study. Learning to write and read German, Hebrew, Latin, and Greek texts was outside his experience. It is safe to speculate that these subjects were new also for many of his white peers. While his Black teachers and educational experiences at Vashon High School in St. Louis helped prepare Pete for college entry, studying languages was new and demanding.

He studied with teachers whom he described as classicists. They had high regard for art, literature, architecture, and music of ancient Greece and Rome, particularly expressed in the Neoclassicism of the Age of Enlightenment. As a young student, he pondered how to transform his study into a means of liberation. He did not want his academic work to replace his sense of self. He wrote his doctoral dissertation in 1975, reflecting on his early years. Pete asked: "What has it been like to live in the African American experience? Better yet, what is it like to be an African American?"[8] While ever conscious of himself as an African American, he concluded that "ethnicity, social class, skin color, and the like are our identifications, not our identity. We are children of God—that's our identity."

His teachers motivated Pete to develop a desire to understand different cultures. They helped him think more about the workings of power in the ancient world, and he applied what he learned to his own life. Early in his academic studies, he entered a lifelong examination of questions relevant to all human cultures—the place of literature, myth, and history in civilization, questions concerning the nature and limits of human nature, domination, and colonialism, the existence of systemic racism, the role of religion in human life, the purpose and scope of social and political organizations, identity within the ethical formulations of the African American family, and so on.

In 1976, Pete had these and other issues on his mind when he organized the first Multicultural Conference for the Lutheran Church in America, a predecessor body of the Evangelical Lutheran Church in America. The conference focused on the practical challenge of walking with others and sought to answer the question, "How do we learn to listen and talk to each other in new ways?" The meeting led to the development of the ELCA's Multicultural Ministries.

While at St. Paul's Academy and College, Pete's introduction to confessional theology was a growth edge. His understanding of God's sovereign grace and absolute omnipotence was formed. He learned about the proper distinction between law (command) and gospel (promise) in God's word. (The central concern of the Christian Message has to do with our standing before God, as blessed or cursed, righteous or unrighteous, under law or gospel, instead of immediately seeking what actions we should or should not do.) He learned about Martin Luther's discovery of Justification by faith through grace and much more.

Concordia Theological Seminary

From St. Paul's Academy and College, Pero briefly attended Immanuel Lutheran Seminary and College in Greensboro, North Carolina. He transferred to Concordia Senior College at Fort Wayne, Indiana. He found the rigors of academic instructions complementary to his preparatory work in Concordia, Missouri. After graduating from the Senior College in 1957, Pero enrolled at Concordia Theological Seminary in Springfield, Illinois.

When Pero arrived at Concordia, he found an institution where "the atmosphere and the context were one." Pero was particularly struck by what Palestinian literary historian and theorist Edward Said described as "cultural imperialism" in the instructional approach and course content. According to Said, cultural imperialism occurs when a dominant community imposes its culture on a less politically and economically powerful community.[9] "We just learned about God from one culture's perspective. And even according to this denomination, God does work with other folks." Despite the problem of "cultural perspective," Pero was appreciative.

> I think the seminary, by far, outstripped my expectations. I had no idea that we had to study that much, that long, and that hard to be a pastor. But now that it has been done, it is very good to know that I can be in a parish with a garbage collector and a medical doctor and still have had enough training to relate to both.[10]

While the academics were demanding, Pete credits the Pero family with providing strong, nurturing support throughout his college and seminary years. Even though he engaged with peers and made the necessary adjustments to life in an academic community, he remained close to his family. Although he expressed gratitude for teachers who helped him learn, Pete did not develop a strong mentoring relationship with a single college or seminary professor. However, Pete's autonomy was not driven by a wish to be isolated. On the contrary, he returns to the influences of his father, mother, and grandmother again and again. Pete's family provided nurturing support to keep him on track. His grandmother believed that Pete had a call from God to be a pastor.[11]

Pete received the same education as whites preparing for the Lutheran ministry. He was, however, sensitive to the discriminatory placement practices of the Lutheran Church following graduation from Concordia Seminary. Pero reflected on ministry assignments: "I could never figure out why, if they expected me to know everything that my other [white] colleagues knew, why then was I not received into a white congregation as everybody was." Pete lamented that when he completed his seminary education, "Blacks could only serve black parishes, while whites could work anywhere in the world." Districts of the Lutheran Church-Missouri Synod regularly assigned white Lutherans to Black congregations in the United States. Nelson Trout was among the first African Americans assigned to a white Lutheran congregation when he was called in 1966 to Grace Norwegian American Lutheran Congregation of Eau Claire, Wisconsin.

Pero earned a bachelor of arts degree from St. Paul's College in 1957 and a Bachelor of Arts in Theology from Concordia Theological Seminary in 1962. He received a master of arts in Sociology from the University of Detroit-Mercy in 1967. Pero earned his doctor of theology from the Lutheran School of Theology Chicago in 1975. He completed postdoctoral studies at the University of Chicago and the University of Zimbabwe. He joined the LSTC faculty in the fall of 1975 as an instructor.

In the early 1960s, Pero did mission work at the Robert Taylor Homes in Chicago. The Robert Taylor Homes was a public housing project in Chicago's South Side. It was the largest housing project in the United States at the time. He later served as pastor and principal at Berea Lutheran Church & School in Detroit and part-time professor at Shaw University of Detroit.

Pero returned to Chicago in 1970 to serve as Christ the King Lutheran Church's pastor. While earning his doctorate, he was a part-time instructor in Systematic Theology and Contemporary Black Theology at Saint Louis University, Concordia Seminary, and Metropolitan Community College in St. Louis. During that time, he also served on the executive staff of Partners in Mission.

Being Black and Lutheran

Pete's college and seminary experiences highlight the difficulties encountered by Blacks in preparing for public ministry roles in the Lutheran Church in the United States. Beginning with Jehu Jones Jr., in 1832, Lutherans had a difficult time with the education and placement of Black pastors. Pete Pero is an example of how those difficulties could be overcome as he was able to complete an education. However, Pete wrestled with being Black and Lutheran. Through the lens of W. E. B. Du Bois, Dr. Richard Perry, a student and colleague of Pero, reflected on Pero's dilemma:

> What does it mean to be Black and Lutheran? People of African descent within Lutheranism experience a double consciousness, marginalization, and invisibility. In the African-American world, we are at the margins because of our religious identity as Lutherans. In the Lutheran world, we are at the margins because of our racial identity as African Americans. This dilemma raises the issue of identity and identification so crucial for African American Lutherans. Pero wrestles with this double consciousness through his theological method and understanding of the human condition.[12]

At the 1986 organizational meeting of the Conference of International Black Lutherans, Pete said, "I have been a black Lutheran all my life. Symbolically speaking, I have been 'Black by day and Lutheran by night.'" In 1985, Pete and Dr. Ambrose Moyo, a Lutheran pastor and professor of theology at the University of Zimbabwe, organized a consultation on "The Meaning of the Lutheran Heritage and the Black Experience in Africa and the Americas." Moyo and Pero were aware of the growth of the Lutheran movement on the continent of Africa. According to Lutheran World Federation membership numbers, membership in the various African Lutheran Churches reached 24,135,465 in 2017.[13] Membership in Lutheran churches in Africa is second to Europe, which had a membership of 33,733,309 in 2017. Pero and Moyo recognized the need for Lutheran theologians of Africa and African descent to meet, formulate, articulate, and communicate their understandings of the Lutheran tradition based on their experiences. The meeting took place in 1986 in Harare, Zimbabwe. Papers from the Harare consultation were co-edited by Pero and Moyo and published in the anthology *Theology and the Black Experience: The Lutheran Heritage Interpreted by African and African-American Theologians*.[14] The collection includes two essays by Pete, "On Being Black, Lutheran, and American in a Racist Society" and "Worship and Theology in the Black Context." At the Harare consultation, Pero proposed the formation of an international organization. As a result, participants at the consultation formed the Conference of International Black Lutherans (CIBL). Part of CIBL's mission is "bridging the relational gap between and among Lutherans of Africa descent; contributing to Lutheran theological conversations; assisting in the development of contextualized theological education for African and African American Lutherans in particular; and nurturing an appreciation for African and African American Christian contributions to the whole church."[15]

Seminary students and theologians looked up to Pete as a model to emulate. He taught numerous generations of students that ministry encompasses not only serving in congregations, doing missionary work, or working in agencies (as crucial as they are) but also actively engaging with the brokenness that exists in the world. Pete believed that the church lives and thrives when it participates in, reproduces, and extends the hospitality of God. One of his notable expressions was, "Let's get real." By this, he meant the church, as Christ's body in the world, comes to life through hospitality, especially to strangers. The church fails if it is content with sitting in comfortable pews. The church, Pete believed, is called to participate in the world's life, shaped by its understanding of baptism, proclamation, Eucharist, offering, prayer, and fellowship. Albert "Pete" Pero died in Chicago on November 18, 2015 at the age of 79.

Notes

1. James R. Thomas. *African American Education in the context of Lutheran Collegiate Institutions Since the Late Nineteenth Century.* Unpublished Doctoral Dissertation, University of Minnesota (1998), 154.
2. Thomas, *African American Education,* 156
3. Thomas, *African American Education,* 156.
4. James W. Loewan, *Sundown Towns: A Hidden Dimension of American Racism* (New York: New Press, 2005).
5. Thomas, *African American Education,* 160
6. Daniel Black. *Black on Black: On Our Resilience and Brilliance in America* (Toronto: Hanover Square Press, 2023), 194–201.
7. Black, *Black on Black.*
8. Albert P. Pero Jr., *Theologia Propria.* Unpublished doctoral dissertation, Lutheran School of Theology Chicago (1975), 135.
9. Edward Said. *Orientalism* (New York: Vintage Books, 1979), 357.
10. Pero Jr., *Theologia Propria,* 160–161
11. Pero Jr., *Theologia Propria,* 158
12. Richard Perry. "On The Spiritual Strivings of Black Lutherans. The Legacy of Dr. Albert "Pete" Pero." *Currents in Theology and Mission* 32, no. 3 (June 2004): 205.
13. "The Lutheran World Federation—2019 Membership Figures." Lutheran World Federation (LWF). https://www.lutheranworld.org/sites/default/files/2020/documents/lwi-2019-statistics-en-20200825.pdf. Retrieved 1 December 2023.
14. Ambrose Moyo and Albert Pero Jr., eds. *Theology and the Black experience: the Lutheran heritage interpreted by African and African American theologians* (Minneapolis: Augsburg, 1968).
15. Frank Imhoff, *Claiming the Lutheran Heritage for Black People.* Worldwide Faith News archives www.wfn.org. https://archive.wfn.org/1999/11/msg00086.html. Retrieved 1 December 2023.

CHAPTER 10

Cheryl Stewart Pero

The First African American Woman to Earn a PhD in Biblical Studies

THE STEWART FAMILY had Anglican church roots in Jamaica, West Indies. Woodrow W. Stewart, Cheryl's father, was from a community near Montego Bay. Woodrow Stewart's family were farmers who processed sugarcane. Olive F. Terrelonge Stewart, Cheryl's mother, was born on April 22, 1921, in Morant Bay, Jamaica. Woodrow and Olive gathered their belongings, bid farewell to Jamaica, and embarked on a transformative journey spanning 1,573 miles to New York City, where their destinies linked. Seeking new opportunities, the Stewarts looked beyond the shores of Jamaica. "My parents' goal was to become a part of the mainstream."[1] Mainstream, it turns out, is more a metaphor than a reality. Many immigrants who preceded the Stewarts to the United States continued to find it difficult to climb into the mainstream metaphor. Cheryl would engage in the search for mainstream meaning her entire life.

Early Life and Education

Cheryl Angela Stewart was born in a private residence in Jamaica (Queens), New York, on August 31, 1951. Cheryl was baptized at Trinity Episcopal Church in the Bronx three months later. She attended boarding school in Kingston, Jamaica, for her primary education, from ages six through eleven, traveling back and forth between New York and Kingston. After boarding school, her parents enrolled Cheryl in Our Saviour's School, a Lutheran Church—Missouri Synod co-educational school in the Bronx. Our Saviour's School was founded in 1942 and established its high school in 1955. While the early years of the school saw an enrollment of predominately white Lutheran students, the school welcomed Blacks in the 1960s as whites moved out of the Bronx. The school was predominately Black by the early 1970s. Cheryl remained at Our Saviour's through high school, graduating in 1969.

St. Paul's Lutheran Church in Tremont, Bronx was within walking distance of the Stewart home. The Stewarts identified similarities between Lutheranism and Anglicanism. The Lutheran Church—Missouri Synod congregation provided a "kinship." The liturgy, music, and Sunday School were familiar. The Stewarts joined St. Paul's Lutheran Church. The congregation's parochial school was an essential part of their decision to join. They wanted a place for Cheryl and Maurice to go to school. Maurice, Cheryl's younger sibling, was five years her junior.

Woodrow and Olive Stewart modeled high standards and placed strong demands on their children during uncertain times. The 1970s were harsh times in the Bronx. Tremont was one of the poorest communities in America, where half the population lived below the poverty line and received public assistance. Crime rates were high. Neighborhoods were decaying. The Bronx was burning, and many of the residential structures in Tremont were left seriously damaged or destroyed. The crisis hit Black and Latino households hard. The Stewarts moved spiritually and physically closer to the church, involving their children in youth activities to help keep them out of harm's reach.

When the time came for Cheryl to enroll in college, she submitted to her parent's wishes. She was awarded a New York State Regents Scholarship and was accepted by Wellesley College, a private women's liberal arts school in Wellesley, Massachusetts. Cheryl entered Wellesley in 1969. She selected a double major in Child Psychology and Classical Civilization. The entering class of five hundred, reached a historic milestone with 10 percent African Americans in the overall student body of two thousand.

Wellesley had strong cross-registration agreements with the Massachusetts Institute of Technology (MIT), Harvard, Williams, and Trinity College. Cheryl did her second year philosophy coursework at MIT. Cheryl was close to the mass protests and violent resistance that met court-ordered school desegregation in Boston. She witnessed the anger of white Bostonians, and while tutoring white and Black youth in Boston, she heard firsthand accounts of how desegregated busing ordered by the US Department of Education affected school-age populations. Of course, American children have ridden buses to schools since the 1920s. Millions of children ride school buses every day, but rarely do so as a means to desegrate schools.

The years at Wellesley College gave Cheryl space to develop her personality and interests away from her parents. "I was a real rebel from jump street. I didn't know the issues sometimes about which I was rebelling. I did not realize during my college years that I was rebelling about my parents' authority a lot and the fact that they kind of strong-armed me into doing what they wanted me to do." In some respects, Chery's parents were overprotective and always wanted to keep an eye on her. "I had few friends because my parents did not approve of any friends outside of the Walter League at St. Paul's Lutheran Church of Tremont (LCMS)."[2] Cheryl persisted through her college years and graduated. Congresswoman Shirley Chisholm was the commencement speaker.

Theological Education and Calling

Cheryl's sense of vocation and calling began when she was young, but it took time for her to identify her life's work. When she was younger, she knew she couldn't be a pastor since the Missouri Synod teaches that the ordination of women as clergy is contrary to Scripture. Cheryl charted her course as she proceeded. While in college in the 1970s, she met Dr. H. Paul Santmire, a college chaplain of the Lutheran Church in America. Santmire explored with Cheryl the type of profession, or work, open to her in the future. Santimire asked Cheryl is she ever considered being a pastor. Cheryl walked around for months with that question and returned to the chaplain with a decision to enroll in Andover-Newton Theological Seminary. "At once, the seeds were sown, and I enrolled in seminary." Cheryl still had traveling to do.[3]

While Cheryl attributed the ideal of serving in the ministry to conversations with Santimire, a ministry vocation needed nurturing. "I think I've always been aware of having a vocation that had something to do with the church."[4] Cheryl established a mentoring relationship with Paul Santimire. "He was very affirmative of my struggle to break loose from my parents to develop my autonomy and track record as well as sort through issues of self-identity."[5] She credited her relationship with Santimire with furthering her spiritual and educational development.

However, Cheryl found it difficult to imagine a white male having that kind of influence on her. She believed it was the power of the Lord at work. "Whiteness and blackness had very little to do with what was going on. It has something to do with where God was pushing me."[6]

In 1973, Cheryl entered Andover Newton Theological Seminary in Newton, Massachusetts. The school was about fifteen miles from the Wellesley campus. Cheryl cites three reasons for selecting Andover Newton. The first reason was proximity. The second reason was that she was comfortable in the Boston area. The third reason ultimately differentiates Cheryl's educational history from that of William Griffin, Will Herzfeld, and Albert Pero. Cheryl enrolled in a seminary affiliated with the American Baptist Church and the United Church of Christ because the seminaries of the Lutheran Church—Missouri Synod did not accept women. "At that point, all I knew was the Lutheran Church—Missouri Synod, and there was no room in the Missouri Synod for women pastors."[7]

Andover Newton Theological Seminary provided fertile soil for building social bonds. At Andover Newton, Cheryl discovered a "climate of Blackness" that did not exist in Lutheranism. Lutheran churches in the United States have historically had a predominantly white membership and remain among the whitest denominations. She met many African Americans from various Christian denominations who provided mentorship and inspiration for her journey. Cheryl studied with Dr. Henry Brooks. Brooks was the pastor of First Baptist Church in Woburn, Massachusetts. He served as professor and director of psychology and clinical studies at Andover Newton Theological Seminary. She also met and became a lifelong friend and colleague of the Reverend Dr. Rudolph Featherstone, an African American Lutheran pastor enrolled in studies at Harvard Divinity School. Featherstone was the first African American to graduate from Gettysburg College, a Lutheran college in Pennsylvania. Featherstone's brother, Ralph Featherstone, a member of the Student Non-Violent Coordinating Committee (SNCC), was killed the night of March 10, 1970, by a bomb blast along with William H. "Che" Payne. Some speculated that the intended target was H. Ralph Brown, the Chairman of the SNCC. Cheryl worked closely with Featherstone in the Conference of International Black Lutherans. She also became conversant with Cameron Byrd, a Presbyterian Church (USA) minister who introduced her to the National Conference of Black Churchmen.[8] Boykin Sanders, who earned a Ph.D. from Harvard University in religion, specializing in New Testament and Christian Origins, was one of Cheryl's faculty members. Sanders lectured on various topics focusing on religion, culture, and politics in the United States, the Caribbean, and Africa. Cheryl was particularly interested in Boykin's work on Caribbean culture, as it reflected her background. For Cheryl, Andover Newton provided a climate for blackness that did not exist in Lutheranism. At Andover, Newton Cheryl was introduced to what being an African American pastor means.[9]

As Cheryl moved into her final year at Andover Newton, she was still undecided about a career in the church. Toward the end of that year, she met Bob Griese, pastor of a Lutheran Church in Newton Center. Griese encouraged her to contact Will Herzfeld, Pete Pero, and Bill Griffin and talk to them about the potential for ministry in the Lutheran Church. William Griffin visited Cheryl in Boston. Griffin reaffirmed that the Lutheran Church—Missouri Synod would persist in its policy of not ordaining women into the future. Cheryl also spoke to Grover Wright of the Lutheran Church in America. Wright assured Cheryl that she was welcome in the LCA. Dr. Pete Pero encouraged Cheryl to travel to Chicago and complete a year at a Lutheran Seminary (a year required then by the Lutheran Church in America for ministry candidates who earned master of divinity degrees at non-Lutheran seminaries) and to make connections. Cheryl's meeting with Pete Pero would also be an introduction to her future marriage partner.

The trip to Chicago proved fortuitous. Cheryl entered the Lutheran School of Theology in Chicago and was affiliated with the Lutheran Church in America. She was now ready to take the crucial final step toward ordained ministry. In Chicago, Cheryl met and established bonds with Earlene Miller, who, on August 26, 1979, was ordained by the Lutheran Church in America. Pastor Miller was the first African woman ordained a pastor in a Lutheran Church in North America.

Cheryl echoes William Griffin, Albert Pero Jr., and Nelson Trout in critiquing the Lutheran educational enterprise. Cheryl opined about the experience at a Lutheran Seminary, "My experience at a Lutheran seminary prepared me to become a good pastor of a White congregation." She credited Andover Newton for preparing her to be an excellent Black pastor of a Black congregation.[10]

Professor and Pastor

In 1980, Cheryl was ordained by Paul E. Erickson, bishop of the Illinois Synod of the former Lutheran Church in America (LCA), becoming the second African American woman ordained in the Lutheran Church in America, a predecessor body of the ELCA. She completed a program in New Testament at the Lutheran School of Theology in Chicago, becoming the first African American Lutheran woman to earn a doctor of philosophy degree in biblical studies. At LSTC, Cheryl taught a popular course on multicultural biblical interpretation. She was LSTC's pastor to the community from 2009 to 2010. In 2013 her book *Liberation from Empire: Demonic Possession and Exorcism in the Gospel of Mark* was published by Peter Lang. Cheryl also contributed significantly to *Luther's Small Catechism with African Descent Reflections*, published by Augsburg Fortress in 2019. She served in the Lutheran Church in America's Churchwide office, in parishes in Chicago, and campus ministry, and was a convener of the Conference of International Black Lutherans. In 2010, Cheryl became director of LSTC's Pero Multicultural Center, named for her late husband, Albert "Pete" Pero (see chapter 9). While she participated in faculty meetings, the directorship was not a faculty position, and she could not vote in faculty meetings.

Cheryl taught courses at Wartburg Theological Seminary in Dubuque, Iowa, for two semesters. These course offerings allowed Cheryl to use her voice and training for what academia had prepared her for. But she still had to convince her peers that a non-white, non-male Lutheran theologian was a legitimate expert in theology. Cheryl expressed bitterness and lament at some of her experiences at LSTC. "I have been overlooked, ignored, insulted, and marginalized by some members of the faculty, mostly white women."[11] Cheryl wanted to serve on the LSTC faculty but the position she accepted there was a non-faculty job. Cheryl felt "overlooked and marginalized." When Cheryl voiced her sentiments, she created discomfort. Tsedale M. Melaku and Angie Beeman write about experiences similar to Cheryl's: "When people of color give voice to the discrimination they experience, they are often silenced by their white colleagues, many of whom purport to be liberal progressives."[12] Her colleagues did not silence Cheryl, rather she felt ignored. Melaku and Beeman found that "people of color are pressured to conform and manage their emotions to suit the comfort of white people, often as a means of professional survival." Cheryl used words that were no comfort to many, with some shying away from what they saw as her forceful, sometimes grating persona.

Additionally, faculty of color dedicate much time preparing to manage student resistance to their teaching, but that extra work is rarely recognized in hiring, tenure, and promotion decisions. Cheryl worked with "student resistance" and undoubtedly lived with an echo in evaluations, assessments, and peer reviews. Cheryl retired as head of the Pero Multicultural Center in 2017.

Cheryl mentored African American Lutheran women and others as a teaching theologian of the Lutheran Church. She formed friendships with global church leaders. Participating in her funeral was Ambrose Moyo, Bishop Emeritus, Evangelical Lutheran Church in Zimbabwe; Rev. Kwame Pitts, pastor/campus pastor at Crossroads Lutheran Church, Buffalo, New York; Filibus Musa, Archbishop of the Lutheran Church of Christ in Nigeria; Ishmael Noko, a South African Lutheran pastor who was general secretary of the Lutheran World Federation (LWF) from 1994 to 2010; Rev. Dr. Beverly Wallace, faculty member of Luther Seminary, St. Paul, Minnesota; and Rev. Dr. James Nieman, president of the Lutheran School of Theology at Chicago. The Reverend Lawrence Clarke, Cheryl's pastor at St. Mark's Lutheran Church in Chicago, served as worship leader. Known fondly to many as "Mama Cheryl," she left a footprint on Lutheran identity. Cheryl Angela Stewart Pero died on October 28, 2020.

Notes

1. James R. Thomas. *African American Education in the Context of Lutheran Collegiate Institutions Since the Late Nineteenth Century.* Unpublished Doctoral Dissertation, University of Minnesota (1998), 185.
2. Rosetta E. Ross, ed., *God's Faithfulness on the Journey: Reflections by Rostered Women of Color.* https://download.elca.org/ELCA%20Resource%20Repository/Gods_Faithfulness_on_the_Journey.pdf. Retrieved April 30, 2022.
3. H. Paul Santmire and Beverly Wallace, "Tributes to Dr. Cheryl Angela Stewart Pero," *Journal of Lutheran Ethics.* https://learn.elca.org/jle/tributes-to-dr-cheryl-angela-stewart-pero/. Retrieved November 23, 2022.

4. Thomas, *African American Education*, 186.
5. Thomas, *African American Education*, 189.
6. Thomas, *African American Education*, 189.
7. Thomas, *African American Education*, 190.
8. Mance Jackson. *National Conference of the Black Churchmen: A Historical Survey*. The Kelly Miller Smith Collection of the Jean and Alexander Heard Library at Vanderbilt University, Special Collections and University Archives, Box: 135, Folder: 1.
9. Thomas, *African American Education*, 191.
10. Thomas, *African American Education*, 195
11. Ross, *God's Faithfulness on the Journey*, 58–60.
12. Tsedale M. Melaku and Angie Beeman, "Academia Isn't a Safe Haven for Conversations about Race and Racism," *Harvard Business Review* (June 25, 2020).

BIBLIOGRAPHY

Anderson, Hugh G. *Lutheranism in Southeastern States.* The Hauge, Netherlands: Mouton, 1965.

Ashmore, Harry S. *The Negro and the Schools.* Chapel Hill: University of North Carolina Press, 1954.

Bachman, C. L., Haskell, John Bachman, and Audubon, James John. *John Bachman: The Pastor of St. John's Lutheran Church, Charleston.* Smithsonian Libraries. Walker, Evans and Cogswell, 1888

Bolden, Tonya. *The Book of African-American Women: 150 Crusaders, Creators, and Uplifters*, Adams Media Corporation, 1996.

Brühlmeier, A. *Head, Heart and Hand: Education in the Spirit of Pestalozzi.* Cambridge: Sophia Books, 2010.

Cone, James H. *Risks of Faith: The Emergence of a Black Theology of Liberation 1968–98.* Boston: Beacon Press, 1999.

Branch, Taylor. *Parting the Waters: America in the King Years 1954–63.* New York: Simon and Schuster, 1988.

Drayton, Boston Jenkins. St. John's Lutheran Church. History of St. John's Church. Evangelical Lutheran Church in America. www.stjohnscharleston.org/. . .id=64:boston-jenkins-drayton. . .Itemid=8.

Drewes, Christopher F. *Half a Century of Lutheranism among Our Colored People.* St. Louis: Concordia Publishing House, 1927.

Echols, James Kenneth. "'My Soul Looks Back': a personal tribute to Albert P. Pero," https://www.thefreelibrary.com/%22My+Soul+Looks+Back%22%3a+a+personal+tribute+to+Albert+P.+Pero%2c+Jr.-a0117878822.

Ellwanger, Walter H. "Lutheranism in Alabama and Other Parts of the South." *Concordia Historical Institute Quarterly* 48, no. 2 (Summer 1975).

Erskine Clark. *Wrestlin' Jacob. A Portrait of Religion in Antebellum Georgia and the Georgia and Carolina low country.* Tuscaloosa: The University of Alabama Press, 2000.

Henry Louis Gates. "Did Black People Own Slaves?" *The Root*, American Renaissance, March 4, 2012. https://www.theroot.com/did-black-people-own-slaves-1790895436.

Jeremy Gray. "The Execution of Jeremiah Reeves: Alabama Teen's Death Sentence helped Drive Civil Rights Movement." February 4, 2015. https://www.al.com/news/2015/02/the_execution_of_jeremiah_reev.html.

A History of the Lutheran Church in South Carolina. Published by the South Carolina Synod of the Lutheran Church in America. Prepared and edited by the History of Synod Committee, Columbia: R. L. Bryan Company, 1971.

Heinegg, Paul. *Free African Americans of North Carolina, Virginia and South Carolina*, 5th ed. Baltimore: Genealogical Publishing, 2005.

Herzel, Catherine B. *She Made Many Rich: Sister Emma Francis*. Friendship Press, 1948.

Isoardi, Steve. *The Dark Tree: Jazz and the Community Arts in Los Angeles*. University of California Press, 2006.

Perry, Richard. "On The Spiritual Strivings of Black Lutherans: The Legacy of Dr. Albert "Pete" Pero." *Currents in Theology and Mission* 32, 3 (June 2004).

Jensson, J. C. *American Lutheran Biographies*. Milwaukee: A. Houstkamp & Son Press, 1890.

Johnson, Jeff. *Black Christians: The Untold Lutheran Story*. St. Louis: Concordia Publishing House, 1991.

Kreps, Ervin R. *The Lutheran Church and the American Negro*. Columbus: Board of American Missions, American Lutheran Church, 1947.

Larsen, Jeans. *Virgin Island Story*. Philadelphia: Muhlenberg Press, 1950.

Lawson-Haith, Juanita, and Susan Ellis. "It All Began with Children: The First Century of Queen Louise Home and Lutheran Social Services of the Virgin Islands, 1904 to 2004." Lutheran Social Services of the Virgin Islands.

Kaestle, Carl F. *Pillars of the Republic: Common Schools and American Society, 1780–1860*. New York: Hill and Wang, 1983.

Lagerquist, L. DeAne. *The Lutherans*. Westpoint, CT: Greenwood Publishing Group, 1999.

Life Sketches of Lutheran Ministers: North Carolina and Tennessee Synods, 1773–1965. Columbia, SC: Lutheran Church in America, North Carolina Synod, 1966.

Martinez, Diana. "A Changing Population in South-Central L.A., Watts," *Los Angeles Times*, January 17, 1991. https://www.latimes.com/archives/la-xpm-1991-01-17-ti-7-story.html.

Meier, August. *Negro Thought in America 1880–1915: Racial Ideologies in the Age of Booker T. Washington*. University of Michigan Press, 1963.

Minutes. The 66th Annual Convention of the Evangelical Lutheran Synod and Ministerium of North Carolina, 1869.

Minutes. The 71st and 72nd Annual Convention of the Evangelical Lutheran Synod and Ministerium of North Carolina, 1874, 1875.

Minutes. Franckean Synod. 1838, 1839, 1840.

Minutes, General Synod, 1845.

Moyo, Ambrose, and Albert Pero Jr., eds. *Theology and the Black Experience: The Lutheran Heritage Interpreted by African and African American Theologians*. Minneapolis: Augsburg, 1968.

Noon, Thomas. "Black Lutherans Licensed and Ordained (1865–1889)." *Concordia Historical Institute Quarterly* 40, no. 2 (Summer 1977): 54–63.

Payne, Daniel A. *Recollections of Seventy Years.* New York: Arno/New York Times, 1969.

Perry, Richard. "On The Spiritual Strivings of Black Lutherans: The Legacy of Dr. Albert 'Pete' Pero." *Currents in Theology and Mission* 32, no. 3 (June 2004).

Powell Jr., Adam Clayton. *Adam by Adam: The Autobiography of Adam Clayton Powell, Jr.* New York: Dial Press, 1971.

Reuss, Carl F. Interview with Nelson Trout. Oral History Collection of the American Lutheran Church, Evangelical Lutheran Church in America, The Lutheran Church in America, ELCA Archives, 1986.

Santmire, H. Paul and Beverly Wallace. "Tributes to Dr. Cheryl Angela Stewart Pero," *Journal of Lutheran Ethics* 21, no. 1 (February 2021). https://learn.elca.org/jle/tributes-to-dr-cheryl-angela-stewart-pero/.

Schuler, Jay. *Had I the Wings: The Friendship of Bachman and Audubon*. University of Georgia Press, 1995.

Sonksen, Mike. "The History of South Central Los Angeles and its Struggle with Gentrification," PBS-SoCal KCET, 2017. https://www.kcet.org/shows/city-rising/the-history-of-south-central-los-angeles-and-its-struggle-with-gentrification.

Strange, Douglas C. "Bishop Daniel Payne and the Lutheran Church." *Lutheran Quarterly*, 16, no. 4 (November 1965).

———. "The Trials and Tribulations of One Jehu Jones, Jr., the First Ordained Negro Lutheran Clergyman in America." *Una Sancta,* 24, no. 2 (Pentecost 1967).

Thuesen, Peter J. "Enclave within an Enclave: African Americans within Lutheranism. 1669–1994." Center for the Study of American Religion. Princeton University. Department of Religion, February 25, 1994.

Thomas, James R. African American Education in the Context of Lutheran Collegiate Institutions Since the Late Nineteenth Century. Unpublished Doctoral Dissertation, University of Minnesota, 1998.

Trout, Nelson. *The Lutheran Quarterly*, May 1968.

Washington, Booker T. *Booker T. Washington Papers*. Reel 288 of Micro-Film Edition, Library of Congress Manuscript Division.

Watts, David. *The West Indies: Patterns of Development, Culture and Environmental Change Since 1492*. New York: Cambridge University Press, 1987.

Wentz, Abdel Ross. *History of the Evangelical Lutheran Synod of Maryland of the United Lutheran Church in America: 1820–1920*. Harrisburg: The Evangelical Press. 1920.

Whisler, Annie. *Sister Eva of Friedenshort: A Servant of Others, for Christ Sake*. London: Holdder and Stroughton, 1947.

Young, Rosa J. *Light in the Dark Belt*. St. Louis: Concordia Publishing House, 1929.

INDEX